WE CAN SAVE THE WORLD

The Uniworld Plan

Metro-West Publishing
Van Nuys, California

© 1997 Robert Greenberg
All rights reserved
Printed in the United States of America
Library of Congress Catalog Number: 97-92661
ISBN: 0-9660931-8-6

Metro-West Publishing
P.O. Box 7929
Van Nuys, CA 91409

WE CAN SAVE THE WORLD

THE WORLD

The Uniworld Plan

by Robert Greenberg

Preface

This book has a somewhat presumptuous title: We Can Save the World - the Uniworld Plan. Does the world need to be saved? And if it does, why do I think I am qualified to specify how to do it?

The premise we start with is that the world is now heading for disaster. At this writing, the United States, and much of the First World, has the highest standard of living it has ever known. Although there is political unrest and fighting in many parts of the world, the major powers are at peace and cooperating fairly well. However if we continue on our present course the next 20-30 years, the world will be in great distress.

My qualifications may fairly be challenged. My background is in engineering, business, and industry and I am not a professional social scientist, economist, or environmentalist, nor am I a professional writer. You will not find soaring prose or the well-turned phrase; much of it will read like an engineer's report.

But the intent is a presentation of ideas, not a work of literary merit. Very few, if any, of these ideas are original. I have drawn on the ideas of others, from many sources, and combined them into what I have called: The Uniworld Plan.

The bibliography lists my source material. I regret and apologize to the authors of this material that I have neglected, in many instances, to specify the exact reference I drew on in each passage in this book. I am deeply indebted to these writers.

Copies of this book are available at a substantial discount for quantity purchases. Please contact:

Metro-West Publishing
PO Box 7929, Van Nuys, CA 91409
Phone 818-779-1363

I wish to acknowledge the valuable help of my wife, Alice, for listening patiently to my ideas, and suggesting helpful changes.

This book is neither the first word or the last word on the subject. It is my sincere hope it will stimulate others to write better ones.

Robert Greenberg
Los Angeles, California

TABLE OF CONTENTS

Chapter 1.
World Government   14
  Why we need a world government • Eliminating war •
  Historical background • International organizations and
  the United Nations From the United Nations to Uniworld

Chapter 2.
Population Limits   25
  Why we need population limits • What size population? •
  How to reach our population goal • How to get popular
  support • Education of public • Birth control research •
  Abortion • Worldwide birth control clinics • Cultural
  changes are needed • Income tax incentives • Transferable
  birth licenses • China's one-child policy • Incentives and
  disincentives • Coercion and enforcement • Possible
  scenarios

Chapter 3.
Conserving Our Environment   42
  Historical background • Balance of nature • Air pollution •
  Destruction of ozone layer • Global warming • Water
  pollution • Depletion of aquifers • Depletion of marine life
  • Toxic waste • Soil erosion and desertification • Extinction
  of animal and plant life • Destruction of forests • Non-fuel
  minerals • Fossil fuels • What can we do about the
  environment?

Chapter 4.
The Search for Utopia   57
  Concept of heaven • Utopian literature • Plato's The
  Republic • Thomas More's Utopia • Edward Bellamy's
  Looking Backward • Aldous Huxley's Brave New World •

George Orwell's 1984 • Utopian communities • The
Shakers • The Oneida Community • New Harmony •
Comment

Chapter 5.
Uniworld Economic System   70
Description of Uniworld economic system • Groundwork
• Advanced computer network - Uninet • Cash-less
monetary system • Elimination of government debt •
Supply • Production of basic goods and services • New
business start-ups • Production efficiency • Production
quantity • Limits on luxury goods and services •
Consumerism and advertising • Marketing gimmicks •
Unjustified litigation • Demand • Purchasing power •
Social security system • Credit in Uniworld • Full
employment • Can we support so many non-workers? •
Why work if income guaranteed? • Labor unions •
Regional differences • Role of Government • Functions of
government • Uniworld tax system • Uniworld tax burden
• Tax cheating • Other features of Uniworld economy
Business cycle • Inflation • Balance of trade and foreign
exchange • Summary

Chapter 6.
Cities   102
City design in Uniworld • City location • Avoiding
high-risk locations • Risk from outer space • Equalization
of cost of living • House design • Home ownership •
Transportation • Living outside of cities • Inter-region
mobility

Chapter 7.
Energy, Food, and Science   114
Energy • Energy uses and sources • Fossil fuels - oil, gas,

coal • Nuclear power • Biomass energy • Windpower • Waterpower • Ocean energy • Geothermal energy • Solar thermal energy • Solar photovoltaic energy • Automotive fuel • Aviation fuel • Food • The coming food crisis • Uniworld food supply • Science in Uniworld

Chapter 8.
Health Care, Longevity, Genetics 137

Health Care • Universal health insurance • Cost of medical services • Cost control • Patient co-pay • Expense limit to age 70 • Rationing of health care • Medical research • Health education • Prevention • Genetics • DNA - the double helix • Human genome project • Heredity theory • Genetic engineering • Life Span Limit • Life span is increasing • Life-span 80 year average • How to limit life span • Restriction on medical treatment • Genetic engineering to limit life span • Death triggered at average of 80 years • Comment on life-span limit • Limit on physical size • We are getting bigger • Advantage of smaller size • How to limit human size • Optimum human size

Chapter 9.
Language, Race, and Religion 159

Language of Uniworld • Advantages of a common language • Choice of a common language • Race and Ethnicity • Origin of man • Races and ethnic groups • Advantage of racial and ethnic blending • Disadvantage of racial and • ethnic blending • How to achieve racial and ethnic blending • Religion in Uniworld • Freedom of religion • Restrictions on religion • Blending of religions • Discrimination

Chapter 10.
Social Problems 175
Crime • Guns • Alcoholic beverages • Cigarettes • Narcotic
drugs • Gambling • Treating addiction • Enforcement •
Prisons and capital punishment

Chapter 11.
Life in Uniworld 186
Political structure • Marriage and family • Divorce and
children • Teen-age sex • Education • Charities • Leisure

Chapter 12.
Summary and Conclusions 196
Alternatives to Uniworld • Why can't the First World go it
alone? • Questions and answers • How we achieved
Uniworld • The choice is yours

Appendix A 216
Bibliography

Appendix B 221
Ehrlich's Fables

INTRODUCTION

The title of this book is How We Can Save the World - The Uniworld Plan. If you are an average citizen of the United States today, 1997, you may not agree that the world needs to be saved. You have a good job, a nice family, the country is at peace, with no threat on the horizon. True there is that fragile truce in Bosnia, the long term tensions in the Middle East, and the usual massacres in sub-Saharan Africa, but as a whole the world is fairly peaceful. Things are pretty good; what is there to worry about?

Yes, things are pretty good at the moment in the United States and in the countries of the developed world. But if we look at certain trends, we will be aware of danger signs. Looking ahead 20-30 years, we will see that things will not be "pretty good" then unless we change course. What we need to do is the subject of this book, a program called the "Uniworld Plan"

The object of the Uniworld Plan is to create an economic and social system that will provide a good standard of living and a good quality of life for everyone now and for future generations. In reading this book, keep the goal in mind. Note we seek not just the good standard of living, the food, clothing, and shelter needs, but also a good quality of life, the joy of living. A totalitarian government conceivably could provide a good standard of living, but hardly a good quality of life.

Note also that Uniworld is not limited to the United States or the developed world but includes everyone - India, China, Bangladesh, Ethiopia, Bulgaria, Zambia, Iran - the entire world. And note also that Uniworld includes future generations.

By including the entire world, now and future generations, Uniworld seeks the high moral ground. But even though this all-encompassing goal may be the moral position, isn't it overly ambitious? By trying for such a large scope, the whole project may be doomed to collapse. Wouldn't it be more feasible to start the

Uniworld Plan in one or two countries first, and work out the rough spots? Then if it appears to be working satisfactorily, gradually expand it to other countries. And much later think about the people living in the year 2501.

The Uniworld Plan is a long-term program that will take 100-200 years to fully implement, but fortunately we do not need to start on a small scale and gradually expand it. Not only do we not need to do it the gradual way, we are not able to do it the gradual way. We must include the entire world from almost the very beginning. And if we can accomplish our objective for everyone now living, it can continue for thousands of years into the future.

The purpose of the Uniworld Plan is a good standard of living and a good quality of life for everyone now and for future generations, but we must somewhat qualify the reference to "everyone now". More accurately it refers to everyone living at the time the Uniworld Plan is fully implemented. But what about the billions of persons that live and die during the next 100-200 years, the transition period until the Uniworld Plan is fully in effect?

During the 100-200 year transition period, those living at the time will receive partial benefits, that will steadily improve over their lifetime. These people do not have the advantage of the full Uniworld Plan, but they are much better off than they would be if nothing were done, and present trend to catastrophe continued.

The first three chapters discuss the three factors that are the foundation of the Uniworld Plan: a world government, a limited population, and a protected environment. When we have accomplished these, we are two-thirds of the way to achieving our goal. In chapter #4, we take a slight detour and explore the quest for a better world in Utopian literature and Utopian communities. The next seven chapters, #5 to #11, outlines the economics and sociology of the Uniworld Plan, followed by Chapter #12, Summary and Conclusions. The appendix has the bibliography, and an article by Dr. Paul R. Ehrlich and Dr. Anne H. Ehrlich, reprinted with the kind permission of the authors.

By referring to the table of contents, you will see the Uniworld Plan deals with a variety of topics. Each of these topics has been the subject of many books by many other writers, so the treatment here is necessarily limited. Few of the proposals of the Uniworld Plan are original; most have been previously suggested by others. The merit of this book. if any, is in combining various proposals into an overall plan, and in pointing out the inter-relationship, the synergy, of the diverse elements.

Some of the proposals are the very heart of the Uniworld Plan, others are less essential, and some perhaps dispensable. As in a house, the roof is more important than the wallpaper. Some of the proposals may appear to you as impractical, or irrational, or absurd and you may be right.

This is not a scholarly book, but it is a serious effort to deal with a serious problem, one that will affect us all, and will not go away. If it spurs you to write a better book, it has not failed.

CHAPTER ONE
WORLD GOVERNMENT

The three elements that form the heart of the Uniworld Plan are: a world government, a limited population, and a protected environment. In this chapter we will discuss world government.

Why we need a world government

We can't limit population without a world government, and we can't protect the environment, unless we can limit population. We can't do this with 185 sovereign nations, debating endlessly. If the United Nations was so strengthened that a majority decision of the General Assembly was binding on every country, in effect the United Nations would have become a world government, but this is not what we have.

Without a world government we will be unable to check the population explosion. Without a world government effective protection of the environment is a lost cause. Air pollution and destruction of the ozone layer does not stop at a national boundary. Toxic waste within one country may migrate to a neighboring country by surface and underground water flow. Waste of natural resources, and destruction of rain forests and wetlands, even if confined within a national boundary, is nevertheless a loss to the entire world economy.

We don't have the luxury of waiting for public opinion to gradually become aware of the problem. Time is working against us. Despite the valiant efforts of many worthy environmental organizations concerned with population and environment, and legislation by many countries, the situation has worsened. The best that can be said is that these efforts have slowed down the rate of destruction, but not stopped it. Only a world government can take effective action.

Without a world government it will be impossible to provide a good standard of living for everyone worldwide, because a huge proportion of industrial production and services now needs to be expended for military defense, for war materials, for repairing war damage, for care of the war wounded, some for a lifetime, and for financial support of family dependents of the dead and wounded.

The Uniworld Plan has many provisions, to be discussed in later chapters, that taken together will make possible a good standard of living and good quality of life for everyone. With few exceptions, every one of these, to be effective, requires a world government.

Eliminating war

A major benefit of Uniworld is the elimination of war. No country will have its own military force. Only the Uniworld central government will have military capability, a small standing army. No more wasteful spending for military preparedness, no more millions of war dead and injured, no more wartime destruction of the economy and the environment.

From the earliest days of human history, wars have brought death, misery, and destruction. Wars have always had a high price, but now the price might be the complete elimination of all human life. Over the ages, science and technology have increased the killing efficiency of weaponry - the English cross-bow which countered the knight's armor, gunpowder, the machine gun, the bomber plane, guided missiles, poison gases and biological agents, culminating in the atomic and hydrogen bomb.

The First World War gave us 10 million dead, World War II, 35 million dead. Since 1945 we have had innumerable wars, fortunately none on a global scale, yet 16 million have died.

An all-out nuclear war between the United States and Russia would kill millions outright, and might so contaminate the air, soil, and water as to threaten the survival of the human race. The 50,000 nuclear devices out there have an explosive capacity of 20,000 million tons of TNT. Just one of the 192 nuclear warheads on a single US missile submarine, if detonated 6000 feet above Moscow, would destroy most of the central city. The US military operation plan in event of nuclear war, the "doomsday book", targets 15,000 sites in the Soviet Union.

Fortunately for mankind there has been no nuclear war, so far. The M*A*D policy, Mutually Assured Destruction, has been an effective deterrent, and the threat has greatly decreased the past few years with the breakup of the Soviet Union. But let us not become too complacent; the nuclear threat has been only temporarily reduced. Nuclear weapon capability continues to proliferate. At present the nuclear "club" includes the United States, England, France, China, Russia, India, Pakistan, and Israel. North Korea, Iran, Iraq and others are knocking at the door.

And we are becoming increasingly concerned about China. Even though communism in China has been somewhat relaxed with more free-market activity, it is still a highly controlled society, extremely nationalistic. Its economy is expanding rapidly, and China is making heavy purchases of advanced military equipment, and is becoming increasingly aggressive in asserting its territorial claims to Taiwan and elsewhere. By the year 2025, it is estimated China's population will be 1.5 billion, five times ours.

Even if all nuclear weapons were eliminated, we are still at high risk from chemical and biologic agents. According to the American Chemical Association, the Pentagon had 5,000 times enough nerve gas to kill everyone on earth. But even if every nation in the world completely disarmed - weapons of every type, nuclear and non-nuclear - we are still not safe. The technical know-how to build these weapons remains. How will we be sure that some country somewhere, led by another Hitler, is not building these weapons secretly?

It's been more than 50 years since the conclusion of World War II, and we have been spared a war between major powers, using modern nuclear, chemical, or biologic weapons. But 50 years is a short time. Society must survive for hundreds and thousands of years. With exploding human population and competition for a dwindling supply of essential resources, what assurance do we have that society will not disintegrate in war within the next 100 years? Our only protection is an effective world government.

Historical background

The formation of the United States government, as described in the book "Planethood" by Ferencz and Keyes, is a useful reference point. The 13 colonies declared its independence from England on July 4, 1776 and fought a war with England until the surrender of Cornwalis at Yorktown October 19, 1781. During the War for Independence there was no United States of America, but rather l3 sovereign nation-states, joined loosely by the "Articles of Confederation". The Articles were completed November 15, 1777, but it took five years until all 13 states signed them.

After the war, the limited cooperation that existed during the war soon began to evaporate in peacetime. Under the Articles of Confederation there was no chief executive. The Continental Congress did not have the power to make enforceable laws, and no court had the power to settle disputes between the states.

To cover the cost of government, each state was asked to contribute its share, but a state would cut off funds if things did not go its way. New York levied tariff and custom fees on goods from other states, even though forbidden in the Articles. The oyster fisherman of Maryland and Virginia were fighting over fishing rights on the Potomac River. Nine states had navies of their own, and all the states considered their militia as a state army.

Seven of the states were printing worthless paper money. When the Continental Congress in 1781 tried to raise money by a 5% duty on imports, New York blocked it because it wanted its own custom system to extract money from the other states. The Pennsylvania army attacked settlers from Connecticut, the Wyoming Massacre, and 2,000 were killed before the fighting stopped. In 1786 many of the New England states were threatening to leave the Union and start their own confederation.

Finally in May 1787 delegates from the 13 states met in Philadelphia for the sole purpose of revising the Articles of Confederation. This was the famous Constitutional Convention. The delegates soon realized that a mere patching up would not do it - a complete overhaul was needed - but it was not easy. The Convention almost collapsed over the demands of the small states to have an equal voice in Congress, and the demand of the large states to be represented proportionately to population. Slavery and the slave trade was another volatile issue.

The delegates labored day after day through a long hot summer to resolve the differences and find acceptable compromises - how to enact taxes, appropriate money, and approve foreign treaties - limitations of the power of all three branches of the government and the President. By ingenious checks and balances it was all summed up in seven Articles. No one was completely satisfied, but the Constitution was a magnificent compromise.

On September 17, 1787, less than four months after the first session of the Convention, the Constitution of the Unites States of America was signed by every state delegation. It would be effective after nine states ratified it. The ninth state ratified it June 21, 1788 and the new federal government went into effect. North Carolina did not join the Union until November 1789 and Rhode Island May 1790, almost three years later, and after George Washington had been inaugurated as the first President. In 1791, the first 10 amendments, the "Bill of Rights". was added.

International organizations and the United Nations

In 1899, Nicholas II, the Czar of Russia, proposed an international peace conference, which met at The Hague. A second conference, in 1907, and also at The Hague, was attended by 44 nations. Unfortunately they dealt primarily with international rules for "humane" conduct of military combat.

World War I, with a death toll of 10 million, awakened nations to the need for an international organization to settle disputes between nations, other than resorting to war. President Woodrow Wilson played a leading role in establishing the 1919 Covenant for a League of Nations, but the United States never joined. A group of isolationist senators, headed by Henry Cabot Lodge, blocked US entry. The subsequent march of events led to Adolf Hitler, World War II, and 35 million dead.

In 1945, shortly before the end of the war in Asia, the United States took the lead in establishing the United Nations Organization, a valuable forum for airing disputes between nations. It is structured as a General Assembly and a Security Council. All the member nations, over 160, are represented in the General Assembly, which discusses and votes on various matters relating to international affairs, but has no power to enforce its decisions. The real power is in the Security Council with 15 members - five permanent members (US, Russia, Britain, France, and China) - and ten temporary members. A nine vote majority carries in the Security Council, but on major questions, such as peace-keeping missions, all five permanent members must agree.

In addition to the General Assembly and Security Council, the UN has set up many related organizations such as the Economic and Social Council, Trusteeship Council, International Court of Justice, International Atomic Energy Commission, GATT, World Bank, International Monetary Fund, International Finance Corporation, Food and Agriculture Organization, International Maritime Organization, Universal Postal Union, World Health Organization, and others. These have been of great value in cooperative international affairs.

The most important function of the United Nations is to preserve peace. With this objective, the UN has undertaken many peace-keeping missions in the past 50 years, with partial success. These missions include Korea, the Congo, Arab-Israel conflicts, and more recently the Gulf War, Somalia, Rwanda, Haiti, and Bosnia.

From the United Nations to Uniworld

The United Nations is not a world government but at least it's a step in the right direction, despite its flaws. The peace-keeping mission of the UN is often thwarted by the single-vote veto in the Security Council. For much of the past 50 years the US and Russia had opposing interests. But even when the UN was able to get approval for action to block an aggressor, the UN had to solicit the member nations for military manpower, equipment, supplies and money. No nation was compelled to assist. The United States, and most other nations, even if willing to help, usually insisted on full control of its own troops, rather than merging into a unified UN command.

For effective peace-keeping the UN must have a permanent standing military force, under full UN control, merging the personnel from the contributing nations, and with an adequate annual budget. Initially this will be additional costs for the member countries, but eventually there will be a substantial saving in military expenditures.

With increasing confidence in the UN's ability to maintain the peace, a small international peace-keeping force of several hundred thousand well-trained and equipped personnel could replace the millions of soldiers now under arms in the separate sovereign countries around the world.

The voting system in the General Assembly must be changed to give it the power to make decisions, not merely recommendations. It has been suggested that important decisions should be effective by the vote of 2/3rds of the members present, representing 2/3rds of the population of those present, and 2/3rds of the contributions to the UN budget, of those present and voting.

When a country disarms completely and permanently it is giving up its most essential sovereign power - the ability to defend itself and also compel another country to yield to its will. Small countries will be much less reluctant to give up this autonomy, since their independence realistically depends upon the forbearance of the international community. But for a major power, such as the United States, to disarm completely will appear to some as a surrender of nationhood. It is feasible only if all the major powers act in concert.

To change from 185 plus sovereign nations to Uniworld, a world government, is a major revolution, and will meet tremendous resistance. Consider how difficult it is for our own US Congress to agree on anything. This will not happen in the next 10-20 years. Meanwhile world problems - the population explosion, destruction of the environment, mass starvation in many countries, terrorism on a vast scale, and proliferation of nuclear, chemical, and biologic weapons - will drastically worsen. Eventually conditions will become so terrible that the major countries will reluctantly realize that the only possible solution to world-scale chaos is world-scale cooperation, a world government.

We will progress from the United Nations to Uniworld in three stages:

Stage 1: complete world disarmament
Stage 2: Uniregions
Stage 3: Uniworld

We start with a strengthened United Nations and an agreement to adopt the Uniworld Plan as the long-term goal.

Unless there is an agreement on the end objective, the Uniworld Plan, we will not be able to even realize Stage 1, disarmament. At the most, we might be able to set up a permanent military force, under the control of the United Nations, for peace-keeping, but it realistically depends upon the support of the major powers. This UN military force is certainly desirable and should be valuable in reducing the risk of regional wars, but it is unlikely this would be sufficient to progress to worldwide disarmament. Individual countries, especially the major powers, will insist on maintaining their own military force, in the event of serious international disagreements that can't be resolved to their satisfaction by the United Nations.

Without complete world-wide disarmament, Uniworld is not possible, and without Uniworld, a world government and complete worldwide disarmament is not possible. So, in a sense, Stage 1, disarmament, and Stage 2, Uniregions, must start concurrently.

Stage 2, Uniregions, is the transition between the United Nations and Uniworld. The Uniworld Plan has the goal of not only a good standard of living for everyone world-wide, but also the same standard of living - Bangladesh and Ethiopia same as the United States.

A key provision of the Uniworld Plan is a single worldwide economy. This would be unacceptable to the United States and the other First World countries because the result would be a drastic decline in its standard of living. Let's arbitrarily assign a standard of living (SOL) index of 100 to the First World and a SOL index of 20 (probably over-stated) to the Third World. Now if the First World at once merged its economy with the Third World, and if the population in the First World was same as the Third World, the merged economy would have a SOL index of 60. However the population of the Third World is about three times the First World, so the merged SOL index will become 40: $(100 + (3 \times 20))$ / 4 = 40. The First World will be unwilling to have its standard of living reduced to 40% of what it was, and with the probability it would be 150 years or longer before it recovered.

Instead of starting with a worldwide government and one worldwide economy, the solution is to merge the 185 nations into say eight groups, called Uniregions, each an independent sovereign country with its own independent economy. Then later, when the economies of the Third World had substantially improved, all the Uniregions will be merged into Uniworld.

An extensive analysis and study will be made to determine the most suitable groupings to make up each Uniregion. Geographic proximity and similar level of standard of living will be important factors as well as enough agricultural land to be self-sufficient in supply of food. Ethnic and racial diversity in each region is also desirable, as will be discussed in a later chapter.

Each Uniregion will be a sovereign nation, make its own laws, manage its own economy, collect its own taxes, pay for and operate its own social security and health insurance plans, and carry out all the usual functions of an independent nation. Instead of 185 nations, we will then have eight Uniregions. Representatives of each of the eight Uniregions would form the new United Nations and would decide on and administer programs and projects that affected more than one Uniregion.

Since the new Uniregions were formed of countries with roughly similar standard of living, the First World countries will be in different Uniregions from the Third World countries, and the wide disparity between the First and Third World will continue. If all the countries had been merged into one, with one economy, the standard of living of the First World countries would have drastically declined. The long range plan is to improve the standard of living of the Third World

Uniregions, bring them up to the level of the First World and then merge all the Uniregions into one Uniworld.

Another major problem will be money. The First World countries do not have surplus funds; most are operating at budget deficits. The most likely source of funds is in the military budget of each country. If all the countries, First World and Third World, disbanded their military forces, leaving only a small United Nations peace-keeping military force, this will make substantial funds available. In some of the Third World countries more than 30% of government expenditures is for the military. Concurrently with the formation of the Uniregions, all military forces in every country will be disbanded.

The First World Uniregions will agree to cancel the indebtedness Third World countries owe to First World countries (repayment is unlikely in any event) and also agree to provide extensive financial and technical assistance to the Third World Uniregions to improve their standard of living as quickly as possible. In return the Third World Uniregions agree to initiate aggressive programs to stop population growth and protect the environment.

Assistance for the Third World will focus on providing the basic necessities of living - food, clothing, shelter, medical care, and education. This includes clean water, sanitation, sound agricultural practices, good simple housing, small scale industry for making clothing, and other projects to improve standard of living for everyone, not just the top echelon.

Although the eight Uniregions will be separate governments and separate economies, with different standards of living, many of the principles of the Uniworld Plan, to be discussed in later chapters, can be initiated at once.

As the standard of living of a Uniregion is raised to parity or near-parity with another nearby Uniregion, the two Uniregions will merge. We may start with eight Uniregions, but mergers over a period of time will gradually reduce the number of separate Uniregions, to 7, to 5, to 3, to 2, and then finally to Uniworld, one world, one economy. Stage 2, the transition from Uniregions to Uniworld, will probably take at least 50 years, or even 100 years, but meanwhile many of the principles of the

Uniworld Plan will gradually be introduced with the United Nations assisting in coordinating the transition. Our goal of a good standard of living and good quality of life, for everyone worldwide, and for future generations, is now possible.

CHAPTER TWO
POPULATION LIMITS

The three elements that are the foundation of the Uniworld Plan are: a world government, a limited population, and a protected environment. In this chapter, we will discuss population.

Why we need population limits

To reach our ultimate objective of a good standard of living and a good quality of life for everyone, a limit on population size is essential. Except for those that still think the Earth is flat and that we are threatened by little green men from Mars, most persons that have studied the question agree that population must not grow without limits. Over-population will overwhelm all our political institutions, all our economic institutions, and destroy our environment.

Our survival depends upon our environment. The Earth and the solar energy from the Sun is all there is; there is nothing else. Perhaps one day we can obtain at astronomical cost (no pun intended) some scarce minerals from the Moon and Mars but this would be of minor importance. We must protect the environment; we can't do it unless we limit population to a sustainable level, and we can't limit the population without a world government.

In 1992, 1,600 scientists - including half of the living Nobel laureates in science - signed a declaration to the world's leaders: "No more than a few decades remain before the chance to avert the threats we now confront will be lost, and the prospects for humanity immeasurably diminished."

In 1798 the Reverend Thomas Malthus , a professor of political economy in England, published "An Essay on the Principle of Population", a short pamphlet. Malthus argued that sexual drives induced people, especially the poor, to reproduce themselves to the point of bare subsistence. Population will increase rapidly at an exponential rate, but the food supply will not keep up due to the law of diminishing returns. The population will continue to grow beyond what the economy is capable of supporting. Eventually the population will be brought back into balance by starvation, disease, and war.

The gloomy Malthusian predictions have not happened, and it began to look that population was not a serious threat. New technologies in agriculture increased the food supply, worker productivity has increased, and as living standards rose, people tended to have fewer children.

But Malthus was not wrong - he was just a bit ahead of his time. It took from the dawn of mankind, about one million years ago, to the year 1800, to reach the first one billion population, but since then the increase has vastly accelerated:

1 billion	1800
2 billion	1930
3 billion	1960
4 billion	1975
5 billion	1987
6 billion	1998 (projected)

According to a 1992 United Nations study, by the year 2050 world population will be in the 10-12 billion range.

Population is now increasing at a rate of about 90 million each year, and this increase is not spread evenly.

About 95% of the forecast doubling of the world population will take place in the poorer countries - India, China, Central America, and Africa. The population of the Third World is becoming increasingly adolescent - 60% of Kenya's population is under 15 - while the developed countries are becoming increasingly geriatric.

Population of Latin America, now about 470 million, at current growth rates will double to 940 million in the next 35 years. In 30 years, Nigeria will grow from 115 million to 285 million, and Iran from 61 to 144 million. Mexico City has grown from 1.6 million in 1940 to 18 million today, and will climb to perhaps 25 million in another 30 years.

Some may argue that population size is irrelevant to our standard of living and quality of life. If we have twice as many people, we have twice as many workers, we will produce twice as much, and per capita gross world product will be unaffected. But this is not true. Classical economics says the basic elements of production are land, labor, and capital. We can double labor, but we can't double land and we can't double capital (water, air, natural resources). Our survival depends entirely upon what now exists here on earth, plus the solar energy from the Sun. We are living within a limited eco-system, and we have no way to add to what we now have.

There are some, such as economist Julian Simon, that say the population doomsayers are like Chicken Little. The world's resources are practically limitless, argues Simon, because of scientific ingenuity. Genetic engineering and super-efficient farming can easily provide enough food for 10 billion. This is wishful thinking. Even if it were possible to feed 10 billion, how long could this continue? Isn't it likely that at this rate of intensive farming, soils will become decreasingly productive? And what about the other needs of 10 billion people - clothing, housing, energy? At what standard of living?

But even if the Earth can support a population of 10 billion, what about 20 billion? Does Julian Simon believe a population of 40 billion is sustainable? Certainly we agree there is some limit to the number of people that can inhabit the Earth at a decent quality of life. The only question we should be debating is how many.

What size population?

The optimum population is not the maximum number that can be fed living like peasants, but the number that can live in a decent standard of living in a sustainable environment.

In an interview in the ZPG Reporter, December 1992, Donella Meadows, co-author of Limits to Growth and Beyond the Limits, states: "We think 8 billion people living at a roughly Western European level of affluence, though with much more efficient use of energy and material than is now the case, is possible. But if the population goes to 12.5 billion, which is likely in terms of current growth trends, we can't make it. Either we have to cut down on lifestyle, or get into the other scenario, collapse."

However a population of 8 billion is not realistic either. The developed world, especially the US, is using much more than its fair share of the world's resources. Each American consumes 23 times more goods and services than the average Third Worlder. Americans consume 570 pounds of dairy products per year, compared with a worldwide average of 170 pounds. Feed grains for food-producing animals are consumed at a rate of 1,460 pounds per capita in the US, compared with 255 pounds for the rest of the world. Less than 25% of the world population is in the developed countries, but they gobble up 80% of the world's production. A child born in the US, during its lifetime will have 30 times as much impact on the environment as a child born in India.

The US has 5% of the world population, but it consumes 25% of the energy. The energy use of the average American is equivalent to the consumption of 3 Japanese, 6 Mexicans, 12 Chinese, 33 Indians, 147 Bangladeshis, 281 Tanzanians, or 422 Ethiopians.

When thinking about population growth, countries like India, Bangladesh, and Kenya come to mind. But population in the industrialized world, due to its disproportionate impact on global resources, greatly affects long-term sustainability. The US with 5% of world population consumes 27% of the world's aluminum and over 20% of its tin, copper, and lead. And we produce much more waste.

If the Third World docilely permits the industrialized First World to continually use many times its fair share of global resources, then maybe - just maybe - we could sustain a 6 billion population. But this is not realistic; sooner or later the Third World will protest, perhaps violently.

David Pimentel, Cornell University ecologist, in a study released in 1992, states that population must be reduced to two billion by 2100. If current trends continue population will increase to 12 to 15 billion with worldwide misery, poverty, disease, and starvation. Lindsey Grant, writing in NPG Inc. bulletin, also advocates a goal of 2 billion. Paul Ehrlich, pioneer population writer, author of The Population Bomb, is another advocate of a greatly reduced world population.

For Uniworld we too propose a stable population of two billion.

Some of us may feel uncomfortable with the concept of reducing world population from 6 billion to 2 billion. Isn't this unfair to future generations? There are 4 billion persons out there that never get a chance to live. Somehow they visualize a queue of persons, waiting patiently in line to be born, and we are denying them this chance to experience life! But in reality no one is waiting out there; there is no queue.

A woman produces about 400 mature egg gametes in her child-bearing years, and the male sperms are in the billions. Potentially we can produce astronomical numbers of babies, but how they could survive is another story. However egg cells and sperm cells are not people. Even the Vatican doesn't count them as people until fertilization. We need not feel guilty; no one is out there waiting to get born.

How to reach our population goal

In the prior section we concluded that our population goal will be 2 billion, but how are we going to attain this reduced number? The present world population is nearly 6 billion, and since we will exclude the option of simply executing 4 billion people, it is apparent we have a very difficult problem.

Our task is compounded by a long time frame. If we make too many automobiles, we can readily adjust by reducing production the following year, but if we make too many babies we are stuck with the surplus for about 80 years.

Population will decline if the number of deaths exceeds the number of births. We can't purposely increase the death rate, but we can purposely try to reduce the birth rate. The most desirable way to reduce the birth rate is by voluntary cooperation, but this is wishful thinking. Even if a substantial majority of the people recognize the need for a reduced population and are willing to cooperate, this will not be sufficient. Total compliance, or near-total, is essential.

Consider two neighboring countries, A and B, presently at peace but historically there have been some less-than-friendly disputes. Country A might be willing to reduce its population, but only provided Country B does likewise. If Country A were to go ahead on its own, it would be at a manpower disadvantage if war broke out between them. It is true than in this era of modern killing machines manpower is less significant than formerly, but recent local wars have used conventional weapons and manpower superiority can make a difference.

Population is not growing in the European countries and in some, Russia for example, population is actually decreasing. Population of the United States is increasing, primarily due to immigration, legal and not-so-legal. But the Third World has a much greater difficulty.

To better realize the difficulty of limiting population consider the United States. In the opinion of NPG Inc., the US with a population of 260 million is already vastly over-populated in terms of its long range carrying capacity. A fertility rate of about 2.1 children per family is the replacement level at which births equal deaths. If the US remains at its present fertility rate of 2.0 and immigration at its present level, this is a 1.0% growth rate. By the year 2080, US population will be 600 million. If the annual growth rate became 1.3% instead of 1.0%, in 2080 the population of US will be 780 million, not much less than the present population of India.

The main cause of our population increase is immigration, about 900,000 a year. Even if legal immigration were reduced to 100,000 a year, and illegal immigration to zero, and fertility rate reduced from 2.0 to 1.5, US population will continue to grow slowly for 25 more years. The increase is due to the young immigrant population already in the country and approaching the child-bearing years. It will peak at 300 million in 2020, and then begin a very gradual decline, but it will take another 35 years after 2020 to get back to our present population of 260 million. And to reduce our population to a sustainable level of 150 million will take another 60 years after that. If it will take that many years to reduce the US population, how much more difficult will it be for Third World and Second World countries. Consider these fertility rates: Argentina 2.8, Bolivia 4.6, Saudi Arabia 6.4, Kenya 7.0, and Rwanda 8.5.

How To Get Popular Support

Any program to limit fertility rate and number of children per family will meet with tremendous resistance. It will be opposed especially by religious groups, while others will view it as a violation of civil liberty. It will be political suicide for an office seeker to advocate such a program. Even a program to ban assault weapons is controversial. Imagine then how much controversy will be generated by a proposal to restrict the number of children. If submitted to a popular vote, 90% would vote against it.

If nothing is done, world conditions will get worse and worse. Eventually conditions will become so bad that the general public will be willing to accept a drastic solution to deal with a major problem. But by this time the world will be in ruins. It is insane to sit and wait for disaster to strike.

The political leaders of the world community must be willing to acknowledge that the constantly growing world population is a formula for disaster, but little will be done. Some countries have made an effort to reduce its fertility rate by providing wider access to family planning, and with some success. But a reduction of fertility from 5.3 to say 3.6 while a desirable trend is a long way from the 2.1 level needed for zero increase, and a long long way from the 1.2 level needed to reduce world population to the 2 billion goal in some reasonable length of time.

For politicians the main objective is to stay in office. Most are followers, not leaders. Public opinion polls indicate how the electorate is thinking, and this is how the politicians will vote. It is called "the voice of the people" and as a general policy it is not entirely wrong. But on the question of limiting population we need leaders, not followers. The general welfare is the proper basis for government policy, but on the subject of population limits the people may not realize what needs to be done. The mother takes the baby to the doctor for the diphtheria shot, even though the baby is kicking and screaming. " I know this hurts, but it's for your own good".

The leaders of the world - political leaders, religious leaders, scientists, leaders of academia, and others - must agree that we must first stop population growth and after that reduce the population. They must be supported by the mass media and molders of public opinion - newspapers, books, magazines, radio, TV, and the Uninet. This is unlikely to happen soon. Probably the most we can realistically hope for is that some countries will try to slow down population growth within their own borders.

Education of public

Even if the political and religious leaders of the country recognize the need for population limits, it is still necessary to get popular support. The conventional methods of directing public opinion will be used - newspapers, magazines, TV radio, Uninet, school programs, church sermons, parades, mass rallies, and similar.

The public must strongly recognize the necessity of population limits and be willing to accept the sacrifices necessary to accomplish it. It is unrealistic to expect 100% support of anything, no matter how meritorious, but we need more than a bare majority. Population news, successes and failures, must be reported regularly in the newspapers and other mass media, with reports of developments in our own country and all around the world.

The support of religious groups is critical. Most religious groups, including the Vatican and Islamic fundamentalists, support population limits. However the Vatican and some other religious groups oppose contraception, a primary method of limiting population growth.

Birth control research

To limit population we need to limit number of births. Since it is not feasible to limit sex - though teenage sex will be discouraged - we need safe, reliable, convenient, and inexpensive methods of contraception.

According to Newsweek (3/13/95) Americans are still fumbling in the dark seeking an acceptable, effective method of birth control. Thirty years ago, the Pill was thought to be the magic answer, but today we have millions of sexually-transmitted diseases (STD) and half of all pregnancies are unplanned. The leading birth control method is now female sterilization (tubal ligation) 29.5%, the pill 28.5%, condom 17.7%, male sterilization (vasectomy) 12.6%, diaphragm 2.8%, rhythm method 2.7%, IUD 1.4%, other methods 4.8% (Source: National Center For Health Statistics 1990).

We also need a long-term contraception method for both men and for women. Norplant is a partially successful effort. Newsweek notes that in 1990 nine major US companies were doing contraceptive research; in 1997 only one. US regulators may be partly to blame for excessive caution. It took Deo-Provera, a progestin, 25 years to get FDA approval. Today the Sponge, not the most effective option, but cheap and readily available, was pulled off the market by the manufacturer because it was too expensive to upgrade its plant to meet new FDA safety rules.

The government should fund contraceptive research and encourage it by tax incentives. There is justification for research to assist infertile couples, but the priorities are skewed. According to ZPG Reporter (August 1994) the federal government spends $97 million annually on fertility research but only $20 million annually on contraceptive research.

Probably the most serious deterrent to contraceptive research is the risk of class-action lawsuits by litigious attorneys. To encourage birth control research, we must streamline the approval process, and we must protect the manufacturer from unreasonable litigation. If a product has been approved by the FDA, lawsuits should not be permitted. If after approval there are reports of ill-effects by some users this information should be promptly reported to the FDA, and literature accompanying the product should include appropriate caveats. Of course there isn't any food, medication, or device that isn't harmful to someone - aspirin, milk, bicycles, etc. However if the reports of serious ill-effects are numerous, the FDA will order the product taken off the market.

One proposal is to require each manufacturer to pay a percentage of gross sales into an industry wide insurance fund. Any user that has been harmed by an approved product can apply for recovery of medical expenses from the insurance fund. The mechanism would be somewhat similar to workmen compensation insurance for industrial accidents.

A related problem to contraception are sexually-transmitted diseases (STD), especially AIDS. Except for condoms, most other contraception methods provide no protection against disease. Cynics point out (facetiously we trust) that we can reduce population not only by fewer births, but also by more deaths, so why be concerned about sexually-transmitted disease? Even if we were completely indifferent to the personal suffering, any disease is counter-productive. Our end goal is a good quality of life for everyone. If much of our economic wealth must be allocated to medical care, treatment, and financial support for people ill with diseases that could have been prevented, there is that much less economic wealth available for the general well-being of society as a whole.

Abortion

Abortion must not be a birth control option; it should be used only when birth control has failed, when the life of the mother is at risk, or when the fetus is severely impaired. Every woman should have the legal right to an abortion in event of an unplanned pregnancy.

Abortions should be legal, safe, and not subject to harassment by militant anti-abortion groups, such as Operation Rescue. Freedom of speech is worth preserving, but this does not justify threats against abortion clinics, doctors, and the patients. The best solution of course to the abortion problem is that contraceptives are so effective, inexpensive, widely available, simple to use, and free of harmful side effects, that abortion becomes a rare surgical procedure.

Another important way to avoid unwanted pregnancy resulting from unplanned sex is the "morning-after" pill. The regular contraceptive pill is apparently fairly effective, and this use should be more widely publicized. More research is needed in this area.

Unfortunately many of the anti-abortion groups, especially those that are religious-oriented, are also opposed to sex education and contraception. Some even view the "morning-after" pill as a form of abortion, a stage in which the fertilized egg is not much larger than the dot at the end of this sentence. This is counter-productive and doesn't make much sense. Since it is not feasible to outlaw recreational sex, the best way to substantially reduce the number of abortions is by sex education and by availability of good methods of contraception.

Worldwide birth control clinics

We must set up birth control clinics throughout the world, especially in Third World countries. Some already have clinics, but it is only a fraction of the need. Much of the funding must come from the First World, the industrialized nations, as a form of foreign aid.

If we are successful in setting up an international military force to keep the peace, the huge sums of money now being spent on military forces and equipment by the 185 or so countries around the world can then be put to better use. The funding of birth control clinics is one such better use.

Cultural changes are needed

There are many cultural factors that make it more difficult to limit world population. Many ethnic and nationalistic groups encourage large families. Some religious groups are opposed to sex education, to use of contraceptive methods, and to abortion for any reason.

In many cultures women are second class citizens with limited educational and economic opportunities. With greater gender equality, empowerment of women, and improvement in their educational and economic status, women will have fewer children. But overcoming sheer inertia and century-old customs will require decades, while the population crisis is now. Some militant feminist groups, in their justifiable efforts to improve the status of women, take the position that the woman alone has control of her body, and she alone has the right to decide how many children she wants. This position is untenable since 90% of population growth will be in Third World countries where women desire, on average, three to six children. However much of this desire for large families is due to pressure from the husband.

Because of high infant mortality in many Third World countries, large families improve the chance that at least some of the children will survive. In rural areas children provide low cost labor. A large family, especially sons, is a status symbol and is usually the only available old-age support for the parents, in the absence of any old-age insurance system.

In many Third World countries, such as India, a high value is placed on having a male child. Daughters after marriage join the family of the husband, but sons stay with their parents and hopefully will provide old-age care for the parents. At marriage the daughters are lost, but daughters-in-law are gained, so this tends to be an even exchange. As women became better educated and as their earning power improves, the cultural preference for sons over daughters can eventually be changed, with difficulty.

In Third World countries, especially in rural areas, the people practice traditional medicine and often do not understand or trust modern contraceptive methods. Providers of family planning assistance must be patient and appreciate client values when making contraception decisions.

Income tax incentives

To encourage fewer children, Negative Population Growth Inc. suggests these modifications to the federal tax code: Starting with children born after a certain date, eliminate the present income tax exemption which now applies to every child and substitute the following:

a. All adults, male and female, will be eligible for an income tax credit, depending on number of children and when parented. This will be a tax credit rather than a tax exemption; an exemption is regressive since it gives the largest tax saving to the high income taxpayers.

b. If one child is born before either parent is age 21, both parents lose half the tax credit. If two children are born before either parent is age 21, both parents lose their entire tax credit.

c. Both parents receive the full tax credit provided they have no children, one child, or two children, and provided no child is born before either parent is age 21.

d. If they have three or more children, they lose the entire tax credit. For each additional child beyond the third, they pay a tax penalty.

e. For low income adults, if tax credit is greater than their tax liability, they will receive a cash payment for the difference.

These or similar income tax incentives will be useful in First World countries, but are of limited applicability in Third World countries since so many of their people are at poverty level and never pay any income tax.

Transferable birth licenses

This idea was first proposed by Kenneth Boulding in 1964, and reported recently by Herman E Daly in his book "Steady State Economics". Each woman will receive a license for the maximum permitted number of children in accordance with the nation's fertility goal. If the goal, for example, requires a fertility rate of 1.7, she will receive a license for 1.7. The licenses will be divisible in units of one-tenths, and units are freely transferable by sale or by gift. If a woman wanted only one child. she could sell the surplus 0.7 units. If she wanted two children, she would buy an additional 0.3 units. The maximum number of children permitted however would probably be set at two or three.

China's one-child policy

The Los Angles Times, in an article 7/26/92, describes China as an outstanding example of a tough population policy. Under the rule of Mao Tsetung, large families were encouraged, and the population doubled. In 1979 after Mao's death, the government, alarmed at the staggering population growth, adopted a one-child policy. The one-child policy is strictly enforced in the cities, and its necessity is mostly accepted, but in the rural areas where 75% of the people live, there is more resistance. Because of the traditional preference for a male child, it's been impossible to strictly enforce the one-child policy in the countryside.

China enforces its policy by a combination of incentives and deterrents. For those that comply there are job promotions and cash awards; for those that resist, there are fines and loss of job. Every village usually has at least one family-planning official, and also civilian volunteers that keep tabs on every women of childbearing age. They keep detailed records of each, including menstrual cycles, and make frequent home visits.

When a couple wants to have a child, even if it's their first, they must first apply to the family-planning office in their village. If a woman gets pregnant without permission, the couple will be fined for jumping their place in line. If a woman becomes pregnant with a second child, she must terminate the pregnancy, unless the first child is disabled or if both parents are only children. The local family official will visit her home repeatedly, even 5 or 6 times, to pressure her to comply.

The Chinese traditionally want to have a boy, in preference to a girl, especially since limited to one child. When the woman becomes pregnant, she'll have a sex test to see if it's a boy or a girl. In some cases they will abort a girl, or hide the girl, or pay the fine, or bribe the official, or leave home and then try again for a boy. As the status of women improve, more families will be accepting of a girl as the only child.

The official policy of course is education and persuasion, rather than force, but coercion is used if all else fails. Women are now having an average of 2.4 children, as compared to 6.0 in the late 1960's. The population growth is still staggering - 170 million people will be added in the 1990's, the combined population of England, France, and Italy. If the population policy is able to reduce fertility from the present 2.4 down to 1.7 and hold it there, the population growth will eventually stop and then slowly decline, but this will take at least 100 years.

Incentives and disincentives

Incentives can be for couples or for entire towns, and can include reduced tax burden and preferences in schooling, housing, jobs, and pensions. Cash bonuses can be awarded for late marriages and for sterilization. Disadvantage is the cost of these programs. Disincentives are the other side of the coin for exceeding the guidelines for number of children: tax penalties, and less favorable eligibility for schooling, housing, jobs, and pensions. Disadvantage is that most of the burden may fall on the children who after all are not responsible for being born.

Coercion and enforcement

Coercive methods that might be used against the woman or couple that exceeds the permitted number of children include: fines;

imprisonment; loss of privileges; public censure and shame; compulsory abortion; compulsory sterilization and vasectomy; requirement that baby must be given up for adoption with no possibility of future contact.

Any coercive method for enforcing a population policy will be branded as a gross violation of human rights and the first step toward introducing a "1984" type of totalitarian world. It is unfortunately true that population control and reproductive freedom are incompatible. Certainly education, incentives, and other voluntary methods are preferable to coercion. It is hoped, that after an intensive educational campaign, the vast majority of people will accept the necessity for limits on reproductive freedom.

In modern society there are many restrictions on individual freedom. Thousands of laws, ordinances, and regulations limit what we may and may not do. They can be enforced in a democratic society only if the vast majority of the people are willing to comply. Most people today will not be willing to accept a limit on number of children, and might be willing later only if they can be convinced it is absolutely necessary. Assume you are a survivor of the sinking of a ship, now in a crowded lifeboat with other survivors, with a limited supply of fresh water, and uncertainty of rescue. You will accept the necessity of rationing the water supply and sharing it fairly. We are all passengers on Planet Earth and we have exceeded the maximum number of passengers that Planet Earth can sustain in an acceptable quality of life. Unless we can find a way to stop the increase of population, voluntarily preferably, but forcibly if this is the only way, our society is headed for certain catastrophe.

Possible scenarios

This is a very optimistic scenario: All 185 or so countries of the world agree that population growth must be stopped at once and will take immediate steps to reduce fertility to 1.5 rate or less. The industrialized countries agree to provide very substantial financial aid to Third World countries to set up birth control clinics and other programs to reduce birth rate. World population peaks at 8 billion and then slowly declines.

This is a more realistic scenario: There is much talk that something must be done to limit population, but it is not until 2010 that a meaningful effort is initiated to do something. All the industrialized nations support the need, and so do most of the Third World countries. However the Third World countries will require very large funding of continuing financial aid not just for birth limit programs but for food, medical supplies, and other necessities for their inflated populations. By this time, 20% of the world population is in the industrialized countries and 80% in Third World countries. To provide this much foreign aid from the industrialized countries would cause a drastic drop in its standard of living, and the people in these countries are unwilling to make such a heavy long-term sacrifice. The outcome is the industrialized countries decide to go it alone. Their population is not increasing and within the borders of the industrialized group is enough food growing acreage and natural resources to get by. A few essential raw materials, not available internally, will be purchased from Third World countries.

This works satisfactorily for a short time, but meanwhile most of the Third World is in chaos. With the over-population comes extreme poverty, starvation, disease, political instability, war, civil unrest, and destruction of the environment. The Third World appeals to the industrialized world for help, but the problem is now out of control, and beyond the capability of the industrialized world to do much about it. The inevitable result is that millions of people in the Third World will attempt to emigrate to the industrialized countries. The industrialized world, even though sympathetic to the plight of the immigrants, will set up strong border guards to keep them out, but they will be overwhelmed by the millions just trying to survive. Nuclear weapons won't keep them out. Armed groups from these starving Third World countries will use unrestricted terrorist weapons - nuclear, chemical, and biologic - in an effort to force aid from the industrialized countries.

Millions die. Eventually the survivors form a world government, try to salvage what is left of the environment and try to build a new better society.

CHAPTER THREE
CONSERVING OUR ENVIRONMENT

The three elements that are the foundation of the Uniworld Plan are: world government, limited population, and a protected environment. In the previous two chapters we discussed world government and population. In this chapter we will discuss environment.

Historical background

We like to believe that earlier people before the industrialized era lived in harmony with nature, but this is not always true. When European explorers first set foot on Easter Island in 1722, they found a treeless barren land. It was assumed this is how it always had been, but recent studies now indicate that when people settled on the island about 500 AD it was densely forested. The population grew to 10,000 during the next 700 years, the trees were gone along with most of the birds and animals. As resources diminished, fighting broke out over what was left until there was little left.

The US Southwest was the home of mammoths, huge bears, and saber-toothed tigers when people first came to the area about 12,000 BC, but in the next 2,000 years these animals were extinct, with only buffalo and elk and other modern species remaining. The Hohokam people that lived in Central Arizona from early AD to about 1400 built an extensive system of irrigation, but their settlement disappeared when the soil became too salty for growing crops. Water used for irrigation contains dissolved minerals that accumulate in the soil as the sun evaporates the water.

The Maya that once dominated much of Mexico and Central America had destroyed more than 80% of the area's forests by the time of their collapse in the 1600s. Loss of the forests increased soil erosion and reduced agriculture productivity. Because of this and internal warfare, the Mayas had lost 75% of their population by the time of the Spanish invasion.

Balance of nature

The Earth is a closed ecosystem on which we depend, as described in Steve Pollock's book "Ecology". At the bottom of the food chain are plants, which create their own food using chlorophyll, the green pigment in leaves. and the energy of the Sun, to convert carbon dioxide and other inorganic materials into plant tissue by the process called photosynthesis. Animals are unable to produce their own food; they obtain food by eating plants or other animals below them on the food chain. In a sense, all animals, including Man, are parasites.

Each level on the food chain depends on the level below it. However since there is a substantial energy loss on the transfer, the number of predators are much fewer than the prey on the level below. Early human beings were part of the food chain, much like any other animal, and were food for larger predators. With the development of tools and the use of fire, humans became hunter-gatherers and moved up the food chain, but the number of humans was still limited by the energy available from the food chain level below them. Finally with the development of cultivated crops Man rose to the top of the food chain and large population increases then became possible.

All substances comprising material on the Earth are here permanently, at least as long as the solar system remains intact. Regardless of how they are used they are not destroyed, but are merely transformed. All living things eventually die. The chemicals of which they are made are temporarily borrowed from the Earth, and at death the chemicals return to the Earth. A group of bacteria, fungi, and small animals serve as decomposers and break down the dead material and wastes until all the chemicals are returned to the air, the soil, and the water, making them once again available to other living things. The decomposers are a vital link in the natural cycle of life and death.

The oxygen/carbon dioxide cycle is another important link in the life cycle. Animals breathe in oxygen and exhale carbon dioxide. Plants absorb carbon dioxide from the air and emit oxygen.

All living things require water. In fact 70% of our body weight is water. An important characteristic of water is that it is an excellent solvent. Plants are able to absorb minerals through their roots, only after the minerals have first been dissolved in water. Animals rely on water in their lungs to absorb oxygen from the atmosphere and water in their digestive system to digest food. The hydrological cycle recirculates the world's water. The Sun's heat evaporates water from the surface of the ocean, lakes, and rivers, forming clouds. When the clouds are saturated the water falls as rain back to the surface of the Earth.

Nitrogen comprises 78% of the atmosphere and is essential in forming proteins and DNA, but plants and animals can not use it in the elemental form. The nitrogen must be "fixed" as nitrate compounds by a bacteria called Rhizobium, associated with legume plants. The nitrates are soluble in water and can then be absorbed by the plant roots. When animals eat the plants they obtain the needed nitrates. Still another bacteria breaks down the excess nitrates, returning nitrogen gas back to the atmosphere.

The Earth is completely indifferent to whether Man flourishes or disappears. The Earth and its environment evolved first. Animals, including Man, evolved later according to Darwinian survival of the fittest, and adapted to the environmental conditions as they were then. The environment didn't adapt to Man; Man adapted to the environment. If the environment changed slowly over millions of years, Man might be able to adapt to the changing conditions. But there are limits - if the average air temperature became 230 degrees, it is most unlikely Man would survive. But even a relatively small change in the environment, that comes on suddenly, could be disastrous for our survival.

Let's now briefly review some of the environmental problems that are confronting us today.

Air pollution

The primary cause of air pollution in the United States is exhaust emissions from automobiles. The combustion of gasoline fuel throws substantial amounts of carbon monoxide, carbon dioxide, nitrous oxides, and nitric oxides into the atmosphere, along with microscopic solid particles.

The risk from microscopic particles is receiving increased attention. These ultra-fine particles, thinner than the diameter of a human hair, arising mostly from gasoline and diesel exhaust, but also including carbon soot, nitrates, road dust, etc., lodge in our lungs and worsen heart and lung illnesses. According to a report in the Los Angeles Times, these particles increase by 26% the risk of early death.

Another important cause of air pollution is the combustion of coal in electric generating plants. Most coal has a high sulfur content so the stack exhaust is high in sulfur dioxide. When combined with the moisture in the atmosphere it forms sulfuric acid, resulting in acid rain, which takes a heavy toll on trees and other plant life.

In addition, chemical plants, paint shops, dry cleaning plants, waste disposal plants, and others add to the air pollution. The net result is smog, a common plight in most large cities, but spreads most everywhere. The smog in Grand Canyon National Park has diminished the enjoyment of one of nature's greatest vistas.

Some efforts to cope with the problem have been made in the First World countries such as catalytic converters to reduce automobile exhaust emissions and treatment of exhaust stacks from manufacturing plants. Electric cars may eventually replace fossil fuel driven cars, once our supply of fossil fuels is exhausted. But as the world population increases, and the Third World becomes more industrialized and mechanized, air pollution will worsen.

Destruction of ozone layer

Ozone at ground level, one of the air contaminants from automobile tailpipes is harmful to our lungs, but ozone high in the upper atmosphere protects us from harmful ultra-violet rays of the sun. Even a small decrease in this ozone layer will substantially increase the frequency of skin cancers and damage to eyesight, but will also be harmful to food crops and other plants. This ozone layer is surprisingly small - if it were subject to sea level air pressure, the entire layer would be only 1/8 inch thick.

This ozone layer is being destroyed primarily by chlorofluorocarbons (CFC), commonly known as Freon, that have leaked into the atmosphere from refrigerators, air conditioners, and manufacturing plants using CFC in their process. Millions of junked automobiles are now rusting away in wrecking yards, and most of the CFC in their air conditioners will end up in the atmosphere. The CFC reacts with the ozone and destroys it, converting it into ordinary oxygen. One molecule of CFC can destroy hundreds of molecules of ozone. The CFC from one old air conditioner, rising slowly in the atmosphere, can continue to destroy ozone for 50 years or more. Reports of a large ozone hole over the Antarctic indicates the problem is already here.

The solution of course is to discontinue the use of CFC and most of the major industrial nations have agreed to do this. Unfortunately the substitute refrigerant is more costly, nor does it solve the problem of the millions of air conditioners charged with CFC scattered all over the world. It might become necessary to manufacture large quantities of ozone and discharge it into the upper atmosphere.

Global warming

In recent years the carbon dioxide content of the atmosphere has increased substantially - primarily from combustion of gasoline in automobile engines, and combustion of natural gas and oil in domestic and industrial heating systems and electric power generation. In Third World countries coal is used extensively as a fuel, and this too adds carbon dioxide into the atmosphere.

Most environmental scientists believe this increase in the amount of carbon dioxide in the air is causing average air temperatures to rise because of a greenhouse effect. Radiant energy from the Sun penetrates the atmosphere and warms the surface of the Earth. The earth surface reflects some of this heat back, but much of this reflected heat is trapped by the carbon dioxide in the atmosphere, rather than being dissipated into outer space.

A vocal minority disputes the contention that the atmosphere is warming. The weather and climate is highly variable and the temperature changes substantially with the change of seasons, in a 3 or 4 day period, and over the 24 hour day/night cycle. Weather and climate follow short range and long range cycles of which our present knowledge is very limited. A shift of say 2 degrees centigrade would be very significant, but is difficult to detect against this highly variable background. It would help if we had accurate temperature records for the past 1,000 years, but even data for the past 100 years is limited.

Some say not to worry about global warming. Even if temperature is increasing, it might be a benefit, not a calamity. Farming areas in the temperate zone would have milder winters, and we could farm land farther north in the northern hemisphere and farther south in the southern hemisphere.

This laissez-faire thinking is really flirting with disaster. Our environment is in delicate equilibrium, and if one key factor, such as temperature shifts, the environment will find a new equilibrium, with unforeseen consequences. Even if farming in some temperate zone areas might benefit, farming in the tropics would most likely be harmed.

An increase of just a few degrees will melt much of the polar icecaps, increase the ocean level, and flood many of the world's major cities, many of which are located on low-lying coastal plains. Of course the encroachment of the ocean would be gradual over a period of years, so residents of these cities would not drown, but it would require the abandonment of these cities and building replacement cities on higher ground. The economic cost would be in the trillions. Did someone say something about look at how many jobs this would create?

Most responsible environmental scientists believe global warming is a real threat and there is substantial evidence the process has already started.

Water pollution

Water becomes polluted when sewage and industrial wastes flows untreated into streams, lakes, and oceans. Even rainstorm drainage flowing over city streets carries with it contaminating materials. The pollution kills fish, plants, and other marine life and the waterway is degraded for swimming, boating, fishing, and other recreational uses.

Water pollution is often the cause of serious disputes between countries where the upstream country is discharging untreated sewage and toxic waste into a river that flows downstream to a neighboring country.

The cost of sewage treatment is high and as population and industrialization increases in Third World countries, water pollution will worsen.

Depletion of aquifers

Aquifers are underground supplies of water, similar in a sense to underground supplies of coal, oil, and natural gas in having accumulated over thousand of years. Fossil fuels once used can not be regenerated in the time span of human history, but aquifers can be restored if used judiciously. Rainfall soaking into the ground will regenerate the aquifer and maintain its level, provided the drawdown does not exceed the amount received from percolating rainfall.

In many arid areas aquifers are the principal source of water for agriculture, domestic use, and industrial use. As population grows, aquifers are being depleted in most parts of the world, including the United States.

Depletion of marine life

Fish, and to a lesser extent oysters, clams, lobsters, shrimp, and other marine animals are a major food supply. Over-fishing and pollution have substantially reduced the supply of fish and other marine life. The supply of salmon in the Columbia River, for example, is a fraction of what it was just 30 years ago.

Most commercial fishing areas are in ocean waters near the coast, above the continental shelf. The quantity of fish in deep ocean waters is relatively small. By international agreement each nation has sovereignty over ocean fishing within 200 miles from its coast line. However the coast line is typically irregular with bays and peninsulas. If nations border a bay less than 400 miles wide, especially if there are off-shore islands owned by each of the countries, the territorial control of ocean fishing can lead to serious disputes.

International agreements have slowed down the extinction of fish by banning certain types of nets and fishing methods, and by limiting the fishing season. Some species of whale (a mammal, of course) have been designated as endangered and may not be caught. But the long range trend is a rapid depletion of the earth's commercial fisheries.

Toxic waste

Toxic waste discharged into the air pollutes the atmosphere, into water pollutes rivers, lakes, and oceans. Toxic waste stored in dumps and land fills may end up in waterways and underground aquifers.

Some toxic organic wastes might be neutralized in time by the action of bacteria and other soil scavengers, but most metallic chemical waste can persist as a hazard for many years.

Nuclear radioactive waste is the worse toxic waste of all, because we do not yet know how to detoxify it. Most other toxic chemical wastes can be treated by high temperature incineration, but nuclear waste is like the monster in a horror film. Nothing can destroy it - not freezing, not burning, not dissolving it in acids or alkalis, not burying it, not submerging it under water - it is indestructible. Only time will render it harmless, and for plutonium this is time in the range of 10,000 to 20,000 years. How can we isolate nuclear waste for 20,000 years to prevent it from entering the environment and protect if from falling into the hands of terrorists?

In the developed world, manufacturing plants that generate toxic chemical waste are required to treat it or pay the cost of having it treated. Unfortunately the high cost of treatment provides an incentive for illegal dumping. Even though the cost is high, it is much more cost effective to treat toxic waste at the source than to clean it up after it has been dumped. The US Superfund for cleaning up toxic waste sites has already expended billions of dollars, and has made hardly a dent in the problem.

Because of the problem of nuclear waste disposal, with no solution in sight, no new nuclear power plants have been constructed in the United States for many years. Unfortunately this is not true for France, other European countries, Japan, and other Asian countries, in which additional plants are under construction or planned.

Soil erosion and desertification

Poor farming practices destroy the fertility of the land and convert useable agricultural land into deserts. These practices include clearing of tropical rain forests, over-grazing, farming sloping terrain while ignoring contour layout resulting in rain erosion, mono-crops that become vulnerable to pests, excessive use of pesticides and chemical fertilizers, and build up of salts in irrigated farm land.

The "Green Revolution" with its use of mono-crops, chemical fertilizers and pesticides, replaced traditional farming methods in much of the Third World, and improved crop yields. However this increased yield was only temporary, the soil is being degraded, and crop yields are now declining. As world population explodes, more and more agricultural land is needed, but most of the remaining land is not suitable for farming due to poor soils, lack of water, and unfavorable climate.

These are some of the recommended farming methods:

a. diversified crops

b. limited use of chemical fertilizers and pesticides.

c. allowing fields to regenerate by lying fallow every 2nd or 3rd year

d. planting of trees within crop fields that will provide edible fruit and nuts and also protect against wind and rain erosion

e. planting of nitrogen-fixing legumes as part of the crop cycle to help restore fertility.

f. conserving forests

g. encouraging research to improve crop varieties for higher yield, hardiness, and pest resistance, but preserving crop diversity.

Extinction of animal and plant life

The animal and plant life of the Earth have evolved over millions of years to adapt to the earth's environment, but Man is degrading the environment. By cutting down tropical rain forests, by converting natural wilderness areas into farm land and then into housing tracts, we are destroying the natural habitat of the plants and animals.

A publication of the US Fish and Wildlife Service discusses why we should save endangered species. Since life began, many plants and animals have become extinct by natural changes in the environment, but this decline has worsened by the encroachment of civilization bringing with it habitat degradation, environmental pollution, exploitation, and the introduction of non-native species. During the 3,000 years of the Pleistocene Ice Age, all of North America lost only about three species every 100 years. Since the Pilgrims arrived on these shores in 1620, more than 500 kinds of plants and animals have become extinct.

All living things are part of a delicately balanced relationship between plants and animals and their physical environment. Many plants and animals have a synergistic inter-dependence of which we may be unaware. Destruction of one specie, by a chain reaction, might result in destruction of many others. It has been estimated that a single disappearing plant can take with it up to 30 other species including insects, higher animals, and other plants.

Every living thing contains a unique reservoir of genetic material of which only a small fraction has yet been investigated. It was a fungus that gave us penicillin. At least a quarter of all prescriptions written each year in the US contain chemicals discovered in plants and animals.

We are beginning to use insects that compete with certain crop pests and plants that contain toxins that repel harmful insects. There are almost 80,000 species of edible plants, but fewer than 20 produce 90% of the world's food. Scientists are collecting wild strains of many common crops such as wheat and corn, to develop hybrids that are more resistant to crop diseases, pests, and marginal climate.

We are dependent on many life forms, mostly small - earthworms to aerate the soil, termites to recycle cellulose-type plants and trees, bees to fertilize plants, soil bacteria and certain bugs and insects to recycle animal and plant debris.

We can survive even if the large wild mammals - lions, tigers, giraffes, rhinos, gorillas, wildebeest, bears, and others - became extinct, but these life forms are wonders of nature and should be protected even though they may have only limited economic value. From a moral and ethical point of view, these animals have an intrinsic right to exist, and it enriches our lives to be able to marvel at these miracles of nature. It would be a pity if your grandson would never experience seeing a living elephant or python or chimp. And the cost is not high; we don't need to feed them or provide housing and social security. We only need to let them live and let live undisturbed in their natural habitat.

Destruction of forests

Rain forests in the lowland tropics are ecologically of great importance. Rain forests are home to half of all species on earth, plants and animals, most still undiscovered. Millions of indigenous people live in tropical forests, once on a sustainable basis. These forests are a rich source of raw materials for agriculture, medicine, and industry. One in four drugs comes from tropical forest plants. Many wild plants are related to commercial crops and have genetic material that can be used to produce varieties resistant to pests and diseases.

About half of tropical rain forests, once covering 3.7 billion acres, have already been destroyed. Despite the abundance of lush green vegetation, tropical forests have surprisingly poor soil. Most forest nutrients are stored in the plants themselves and not in the soil. Land cleared by slash-and-burn supports a farmer for a year or two before the soil is dead and the farmer is forced to relocate elsewhere and repeat the destructive process. Forests are being cut down for timber, paper pulp, and fuel wood much faster than they can be regenerated.

Forests protect watersheds, regulate water flow, prevent soil erosion, and avoid sedimentation of rivers. They moderate air temperature, and maintain the hydrological cycle by absorbing rainfall and releasing moisture to the atmosphere and maintain the carbon dioxide/oxygen cycle by taking in carbon dioxide and releasing oxygen through photosynthesis.

Non-fuel minerals

In thinking about conservation of non-renewable resources, we focus primarily on fossil fuels, but there are other essential materials - iron, copper, nickel, chromium, platinum, etc. Most of these have no non-metallic substitute. Automobile engines are now made of steel or aluminum, but can they be made of organic-based plastics?

Even though some of these metals may be a fairly sizable part of the earth's crust, they can be made available only in those few places where they are naturally concentrated as an economic deposit in the form of an oxide or other metallic compound. This deposit is then mined and chemically processed to produce the elemental metal, and subsequently manufactured into various products.

When these metal products are worn out and no longer serviceable, we need to conserve the material by recycling. However even if we recycle all metal products we will not have full recovery. Metal products wear by friction and rust, and the surface gradually disintegrates and flakes off. The iron in iron oxide rust is not destroyed - it is still there - but it is dispersed over the surface of the earth, and is no longer available to economic recovery.

Known ore deposits will gradually be depleted, and we will need to locate and mine deeper deposits at higher economic cost. At current rates of consumption world copper reserves will be depleted in 41 years, and nickel reserves in 66 years. According to writer Jeremy Rifkin, by 2050 the US will have exhausted recoverable domestic reserves of tin, columbian, fluorite, sheet mica, high grade phosphorus, strontium, mercury, and chromium. If we recycle fully, avoid non-essential uses, develop substitute renewable material where possible, we might be able to manage this resource satisfactorily for some time yet, but eventually the economic supply will be exhausted. In the long run we will need to depend on substitutes, possibly carbon- or silicon-based, but the best substitute may fall far short of the original metal-based material.

Fossil fuels

Fossil fuels - oil, natural gas, and coal - are the remains of plants and animals that lived millions of years ago. The most valuable, oil, is the source of gasoline and jet fuel and the feedstock for the petro-chemical industry in the manufacture of plastics and thousands of other chemical products. At the present rate of consumption, proven reserves will last about 30 years.

Natural gas, primarily methane, is a relatively clean-burning fuel, creating less pollution than oil or coal. It is used primarily in stationery heaters, in electric generating power plant, and to some extent in motor vehicles. World reserves are estimated as a 60 year supply.

Coal, in larger supply than oil or natural gas, has uses similar to natural gas. However the combustion of coal, most of which has considerable sulfur content, generates sulfur dioxide that pollutes the atmosphere and causes acid rain. The burning of all of these fossil fuels contributes to air pollution, smog, acid rain, carbon dioxide build-up, and global warming.

With more efficient prospecting technology, we will discover new reserves, but eventually all economic reserves will be exhausted. The fossil fuels are non-renewable and need to be replaced by substitutes. As long as possible oil should be conserved for use as a feedstock for the plastic and chemical industry, and not simply burned as a fuel for heating or energy. It will be difficult to develop a satisfactory substitute for oil as a chemical feedstock and as an aviation fuel.

What can we do about the environment?

We have touched briefly on the many environmental problems: global warning; destruction of ozone layer; pollution of air, water, and soil; depletion of our forests, fish and other animal life, top soil, minerals, and fossil fuels.

Except for the energy from the Sun and the gravitational pull of the Moon, the Earth is a closed eco-system. Our survival depends upon what we have here now. As Paul Ehlich describes it, humanity is living on inherited capital - fossil fuels, high grade mineral ores, rich agricultural soils, groundwater stored up during the ice ages, and millions of plant and animal species. This took billions of years to assemble, but it is now being squandered in decades. It is conceivable we can obtain some minerals from the Moon or from Mars in the remote future, but the economic cost would be prohibitive. And even if this were feasible, we would eventually exhaust that supply also. Then where would we go? To Venus and Mercury?

Except for the millions starving in sub-Saharan Africa, in

Bangladesh, and other countries in south Asia, most of the rest of the world is getting by. However we are consuming our environmental capital and before long we will be in serious trouble. We are already on the downslope and the deterioration of the world will accelerate. Those of us, living in the First World, age 50 and older, will not suffer greatly. By the year 2050 or so when the world is in a state of total collapse we will have already departed for greener pastures. The calamity will descend on our children and grandchildren.

Our environment can not sustain a 6 billion population and it certainly can not sustain the 12 billion population that we will have by the year 2050. Our survival depends on the protection of our environment, the ecosystem of the Earth. To conserve our environment, population must be quickly reduced to two billion and we must have an effective world government. Neither will happen soon enough to avoid a major disaster that will threaten the survival of mankind.

The Earth has been parceled out into 185 or so sovereign nations. To make the drastic reduction from the present population of 5.7 billion to 2 billion will require virtually total cooperation of all 185 nations. We can call an emergency international conference of all the nations, discuss the seriousness of the problem, and all the nations agree to cooperate and in fact do take prompt actin to meet the population goal. This is how it might happen in dreamworld, but not in the real world. It will not be possible to get universal voluntary cooperation, or anything near it. Many think it is a non-problem. Others will contend we can expand the world economy and with the help of advanced technology provide a good standard of living even if a 12 billion population. Others say there may be a future problem, but now their priority is to take care of those now living and not worry yet about unborn generations who will in any event find a way to take care of themselves. It is not until we have reached a state of complete world chaos that agreement might be possible.

We can not rely on voluntary cooperation of 185 sovereign nations to effectively reduce population and effectively protect the environment. It requires a world government with the authority to enforce universal compliance. But unfortunately the world is not ready for a world government - not until the environment has been devastated by a 12 billion population.

CHAPTER FOUR
SEARCH FOR UTOPIA

The first three chapters dealt with the three elements that are the foundation of the Uniworld Plan: a world government, a limited population, and a protected environment. With that foundation we can then design an economic and social system capable of providing a good standard of living and quality of life for everyone.

Our goal is to describe a better world society and how we might attain it. This same objective has been the subject of the writings of philosophers, economists, and theologians for hundreds of years, so perhaps we can find some guidance in this literature, utopian literature in particular.

The dictionary defines "utopia" as "an imaginary political and social system in which relationships between individuals and the State are perfectly adjusted". The word is taken from the title of a book written by Sir Thomas More in 1516 describing a mythical island nation with a perfect society. The term utopian also has the connotation of ideal but impractical.

Uniworld does not have the lofty aspiration of creating a perfect society - but rather a less ambitious goal, a better society. As a starting point it seems appropriate to first take a brief look at some of the utopian literature. We do not expect to find a blueprint in prior literature that we can copy for a 21st century society, but perhaps we can find some guidance in the literature that will suggest a way we can approach this task and hopefully avoid some of the pitfalls.

We will briefly explore the concept of heaven, several examples of utopian literature, and some real-life efforts to build a utopian community.

Concept of Heaven

The most perfect status we can visualize is heaven, free of all earthly restraints. The usual concept of heaven is the place where the blessed dead dwell in the hereafter.

Islam recognizes seven heavens known as the abodes of rest, peace, and eternity and as the gardens of Pleasure, Refuge, and Eden. Heaven is a place of carnal pleasure as well as of spiritual bliss.

Buddhism has many levels of heaven representing gradated states of being. The six lowest are places of sensuous desire and form. The 16 middle levels are characterized by an absence of sensuous desire, but the presence of form. In the four highest, there is neither sensuous desire nor form.

Christianity generally avoids doctrinal descriptions. According to St. Paul, with the dissolution of the body, man instantly quits his earthly "tabernacle" and is transformed to the perfection of the heavenly abode. Eastern Orthodox theology conceived of an intermediary step between death and the ultimate stage of either blessedness or damnation. To most modern Christian theologians heaven is a state rather than a place, a personal fulfillment in God without the popular graphic imagery of angels and harps.

Suppose you were asked to draw up the specifications for heaven and it can be anyway you want it to be. How would you design heaven? Most of us will find it difficult to conceive of anything that is completely different from what we have in our earthbound experience. We will perhaps conceive of ourselves as about 35-40 years of age, happily married to an attractive spouse, with two children aged 11 and 8. Our home, our clothes, our car will be similar to what we now have, though perhaps a notch or two higher on the price scale. We have a substantial income whether we work or not. We are in perfect health, have many friends, and all the leisure time we want. Our sex life is great. We participate in many sports, painting, music, and philosophical discussions, all at a high level of competence. There is no crime, no violence. no poverty. Everyone is happy and healthy and no one grows older. And all this goes on forever. This heaven is very similar to Earth, except it is an earth without problems. One difference is that we will be able to fly like Superman.

There is a TV story by Rod Serling about Wes, a 35 year old man that was killed in an auto accident. In the hereafter he is met by a guide who says he will grant any wish that Wes wants. Wes says he is an avid fisherman and is immediately whisked to an inviting lake. He cast his line into the water and immediately hooks a 5-pound bass. This is great!

He rebaits the hook, casts the line, and immediately hooks another 5-pound bass. Never had he experienced such great fishing! He continued fishing with the same result. No sooner had the line touched the surface of the water, he hooked a fish.

After an hour of this sensational fishing, Wes wanted to do something different. He said to the guide he enjoyed gambling and immediately found himself in a busy casino at the roulette wheel. He placed a modest bet on number 18, the wheel spun and stopped at 18. He had won! He put a larger bet on number 23 and again he won. Now he was more confident and increased the amount he bet. Regardless of what number he bet on, the roulette wheel stopped at that number. He could not lose and his winnings piled up.

But eventually Wes decided he want to try something else. He asked the guide if there is any place he could meet some attractive girls and immediately found himself at a party with dozens of gorgeous young girls. As soon as the girls saw him everyone ran toward him and he was virtually mobbed with hugs and kisses. With difficulty he escaped.

After reaching a quiet area, Wes exclaimed "I didn't know heaven was like this!" The guide replied "This is not heaven; this is hell".

A heaven without problems, without challenges to be overcome, for must of us would be eternal boredom, rather than eternal bliss. However there is no risk that Uniworld will be problem-free. We do not expect perfection; we are striving for a society that is better than what we have now.

Utopian Literature

Dreams of a better world, free of the imperfections that hamper earthlings, are as old as history. Often they take the form of religious or utopian beliefs in a glorious afterlife, reserved mainly for heroes worthy of lasting reward. Thus, Homer's Elysian Fields, Plutarch's Island of the Blest, the El Dorado of Spanish longing, the Happy Hunting Ground of the American Indians, and the Shangri-La of popular fiction. In this section we will comment briefly on some examples of Utopian literature: Plato's The Republic, Thomas More's Utopia, Edward Bellamy's

Looking Backward, Aldous Huxley's Brave New World, and George Orwell's 1984.

Plato's The Republic

The Republic of Plato, written in the fourth century BC, a great treatise on political philosophy, has influenced western thought on questions of justice, rule, obedience, and the good life. The work is divided into 10 books, or chapters, written as a dialogue with Socrates as the main character. After an extended discussion of a definition of justice, Socrates constructs the idea of an ideal state, one which exhibits justice, to clarify the idea of justice. The ideal state needs three classes of citizens: the Guardians, who rule and advise the rest; the Auxiliaries, who provide military protection for the state; and the Workers, who provide the food and clothing and other needed materials. In a just state these three classes of citizens function together, each doing its own task without interfering with the task of the other two classes.

Applying this idea to the individual, the just man is one in whom the three elements of his nature - the rational, the spirited, and the appetitive - are in harmony.

To discover those citizens best suited to be Guardians, the ideal state will educate all its citizens in music and gymnastics, continually observing them to decide the sort of occupation for which they are best suited. In the ideal state, the classes are carefully built up by controlled breeding, education, and selection. Guardians may be women as well as men. Society is communized to eliminate quarrels about personal property. The Guardians must combine political power, intellectual wisdom, and most of all philosophy so that justice may prevail. The Republic closes with Socrates reaffirmation of his conviction that only the just man is truly happy, for only he harmonizes reason, appetite, and spirit.

Thomas More's Utopia

Since the time of Plato men have been thinking about how to make a better world, an earthly paradise. Thomas More's Utopia, written in 1516 in England, in a period of turbulent political strife, reflects the influence of Plato. The English word "Utopia" is derived from a Greek word that means "nowhere". Thomas More invented the term and applied it to a mythical community and then used his account of this community to criticize existing English social and political practices.

In this narrative, More tells of a meeting in Antwerp he had with an ocean explorer named Raphael Hythloday. Raphael claimed he was with Amerigo Vespucci on his voyages to America, and it was on one of these voyages that Raphael discovered the fabled land of Utopia, somewhere in the ocean near the Western Hemisphere.

As described by Raphael, the mythical land of Utopia is an island kingdom about 150 miles in diameter, separated by a man-made channel from war-like neighbors. The island is divided into 54 counties, each with its own town, and no town more than a day's walking from its neighbors.

The government is relatively simple. Each unit of 30 families is ruled by one man chosen by annual election. Each ten groups of families elects a member of the island council. The council in turn elects the prince, the island's nominal ruler, who serves for life, unless deposed because of tyranny. The council meets every 3 days to take up matters of consequence, but no decision is made the same day the matter is advanced, to avoid decisions made in haste.

Everyone works, each man having a trade or craft, except the unusually talented are selected for training and service in the Academy of Learning. The work day is six hours long. All the goods are community owned. Since everyone works, there is more than enough food and other necessities to go around. The tastes of the people are simple, and even the prince shares same as the people. Clothes are simple, durable, and free of elaborate ornamentation. There is no desire for silver, gold, and jewelry.

Violence and bloodshed has been done away with. Lest bloodshed of any kind corrupt the people, only slaves slaughter the cattle. For recreation the people garden, improve their home, attend lectures and concerts, and converse with friends, but gambling is unknown. Although not required, most of the people eat in the community mess hall, where slaves prepare the meals under the supervision of the wives. Spacious hospitals are available in every town. If the illness is painful and incurable priests consult with the patient about the choice of hastening death.

Criminals are enslaved, but not put to death. Adultery is regarded as a crime and punished by slavery. Marriage for love is encouraged, but so is prudence in selecting a mate. Men must be 22 and women 18 before marriage is permitted. Welfare of the family is a state matter since the family is the basic unit of the Utopian state. The Utopians are a religious and tolerant people; some are Christians, but other religions have equal status.

The people want the commonwealth to be prosperous, not only to provide their own needs generously, but to provide funds to buy off their enemies and to hire mercenaries. In this way Utopia can avoid direct involvement in war.

This description of the good life in mythical Utopia is then contrasted with the real world of 16th century England: wide-spread poverty and malnutrition, child labor, working hours from dawn to late at night, hanging for minor theft, high prices, persecution for religious heresy. It is remarkable how many of the elements of More's mythical Utopia are found today in the more progressive countries.

Edward Bellamy's Looking Backward

This book of fiction was first published in 1888. The locale is Boston in the year 1887 and the chief character is Julian West, unmarried, about 30 years of age. Since he was a very light sleeper he had built a sound-proof bedroom with thick cement walls in the basement of his home. He awoke one morning and discovered it was now the year 2000, and he had been asleep for 113 years. Because he had been in a hypnotic state, he had not aged. During the last night he remembered, his house had burned down except for the sealed room in which he slept, and apparently everyone assumed he had died in the fire.

We won't dwell here on the story line of the book, but rather on Bellamy's description of Boston in the year 2000. The city was beautiful with attractive buildings and spacious parks. The air was free of smoke because all heating was by electricity.

The strikes and labor troubles of the 19th century, resulted in a bloodless revolution and a socialist government. No money was used. The state gave everyone a card which contained credit for a year's expense, the same amount to everyone. Store shelves only had samples. You made your selection and the items were delivered directly to your home from a central warehouse. Public libraries were widespread throughout the city. Music was carried into all homes over telephone lines.

Everyone was given a full education until age 21. From there he worked 3 years in some menial type of work. After 3 years, he was given an examination to qualify for a professional school. If he failed to qualify for professional training, he could find other work for which he was suited. Regardless of type of work, everyone received the same annual credit.

Crime was treated as a mental disease, and criminals were put in mental hospitals instead of prisons. Since it was a cash-less economy and since everyone was assured of an adequate living income, the crime rate was very low.

The time Bellamy wrote this book was an exceedingly troublesome period: agrarian unrest, Jim Crowism, strikes, labor unrest, violence, giant business monopolies, widespread political corruption. For an equitable, just, and humane society Bellamy proposed a socialized state whose guiding principle is equality. Everyone is educated to his maximum potential, everyone works at his best capability, everyone receives the same income.

Looking Backward is considered to be America's premier utopian novel and was second in readers in its time only to Harriet Beacher Stowe's Uncle Tom's Cabin. It inspired the formation of 150 "Bellamy" clubs and strengthened the Populist cause and government regulation of banking, commerce, utilities, transportation, and monopolies.

Aldous Huxley's Brave New World

Brave New World is one of the best known fictional works portraying the negative side of utopia, sometimes referred to as dystopia. Huxley wrote Brave New World in 1931 before Hitler came to power in Germany, and before Joseph Stalin started the purges that killed millions of people in the Soviet Union. In 1958 Huxley himself said if he had written this book later his imaginary dictatorship would have been much more brutal. Reality was worse than fiction.

This "brave new world" is a society in which technology has run amuck. The story opens in London some 600 years in the future. Centuries before, civilization had been destroyed in the Nine Years' War. Out of the ruins grew the World State, an all powerful government.

All babies are developed in bottles, none in a mother's womb. An ovary is surgically removed from a woman, kept alive artificially, producing ova. After fertilization by a laboratory procedure, the egg is placed in a solution in a large bottle. By a so-called Bokanovsky budding process one fertilized egg is turned into 96 cloned embryos. As many as 15,000 virtually identical brothers and sisters can be produced from a single ovary. Identical clones will make a stable community without conflict.

Each cloned embryo is developed in a separate bottle, traveling slowly over a conveyor belt for 267 days (approximately 9 months) before it is decanted (i.e. removed from the bottle). During the 267 days, the embryo's class status is biologically and chemically engineered to become either an Alpha Plus Intellectual, Beta, Gamma, Delta, or Epsilon Minus Moron. Alpha embryos receive the most oxygen in order to develop the best brains. Epsilons receive the least oxygen since they will be doing simple manual work requiring little intelligence.

Delta babies are conditioned by Pavlovian techniques to dislike books. If they read the wrong things, it threatens social stability. By sleep-teaching techniques each class is conditioned to love the system and its place in it. There are no families, sex is a recreational game, and everyone is expected to be promiscuous. All painful emotions are eliminated.

Five centuries before, the perfect drug, called soma, had been developed by a team of 2000 pharmacologists and biochemists. Soma is the perfect happiness pill, without a hangover. There is no old age;

everyone remains youthful until they reach their sixties and then die quickly.

Some of the themes that make Brave New World anti-utopian are: individual freedom is sacrificed for stability; misuse of science, genetic engineering, and psychological conditioning; pursuit of happiness, including use of drugs, carried to an extreme; cheapening of sexual pleasure; mindless consumption and diversions; destruction of the family; denial of death. Presumably this society has a good side: no war, no poverty, little disease or social unrest. There may be minimum social unrest in this brave new world because of controlled mind conditioning, but the case for elimination of war and poverty is not really developed.

George Orwell's 1984

This work published in 1949 is an outstanding political satire depicting a completely totalitarian society. The locale is London, the time is 1984, the lead character is Winston Smith, age 39, single, and employed in a minor job at the Ministry of Truth.

The world of 1984 is one in which constant warfare is the price of a bleak prosperity. The Party keeps itself in power by complete control over man's actions and thoughts. As the lovers Winston Smith and Julia learn when they try to evade the Thought Police, the Party can smash the last impulse of love, the last flicker of individuality.

Every gesture, every attitude is monitored by the omnipresent Big Brother. Newspeak, the official language, and Doublethink, holding two contradictory beliefs in one's mind simultaneously and accepting both of them, manifest the devastation of judgment. You feel free because there is no longer any awareness of the discrepancy between truth and falsehood. And then the slogans: Hate is Love, War is Peace, Freedom is Slavery, Ignorance is Strength.

The four ministries of the government are: the Ministry of Peace which concerns itself with war, the Ministry of Truth with lies, the Ministry of Love with torture, and the Ministry of Plenty with starvation.

Every word and every action is monitored by the omnipresent telescreen. Winston Smith's little rebellion is crushed. "Now everything was all right, the struggle was finished. He had won the victory over himself. He loved Big Brother".

Utopian Communities

In the previous section we touched on some examples of utopian and anti-utopian literature. In this section we will discuss some of the real-life attempts to found a utopian community, primarily in the United States. The earlier settlers in the United States were not seeking utopia, but rather religious freedom or economic gain. The problems of industrialization in mid-19th century Europe inspired ideas of human betterment. Robert Owen's ideal industrial community and Fourier's phalanxes became blueprints for utopian communities in the United States. After the Civil War, utopian plans were largely home-grown.

Utopian societies are divided between the religious and the secular, and according to the nature of their economies. Communism, in which all property is held in common, is the most usual kind of economy, but some were cooperative, and a few capitalistic. The religious communities were generally quite authoritarian, with a strong leader, while the secular communities were typically more democratic.

Relatively few of the immigrants to the United States after 1850 were interested in experimental communities. Mostly they were seeking personal economic opportunity.

Most of the utopian communities arose in the British colonies in North America and in the United States, for a number of reasons. First, non-conformists - religious, political, and economic - were forced to leave Europe and seek haven elsewhere. Second, there was an abundance of cheap land in the New World. Third, there was a tradition of toleration for non-conformists, especially in the Middle Atlantic colonies.

America was seen as a haven for utopian societies. The early ones drew their inspiration from the Christian religion using the Bible as their spiritual guide, and the communism of the early Christian church as the model for their political-economic organization. Seventeenth century Europe was full of heretical Christian separatist sects. Once America was colonized, many of these groups fled to the new land. Because of William Penn's benign and tolerant Quaker rule, Pennsylvania in particular was a magnet for many of these religious societies.

The utopian communities in the United States were primarily motivated by religion, but since they had to make provision for a livelihood, they were also involved with economic planning. The religiously motivated communities had greater staying power than the secular communities whose main concern was building a more equitable economic order, because the former usually succeeded better in controlling human greed and selfishness. We will briefly discuss a few of these communities.

The Shakers

Shakers, a Christian sect, conducted one of the most successful experiments in religious communal living in 19th century America. Its founder was Ann Lee, a member of a group of English Quakers, and its first settlement was in Watervliet, N.Y. about 1780. Shakerism reached its peak of development between 1830 and 1850 with 20 Shaker societies in various states from Maine to Florida, and a total membership of about 6,000 persons. After the Civil War, Shakerism began to decline, and by the 1970's was virtually extinct.

The Shakers acquired their nickname from their religious practice of sitting in silent meditation until overcome by a spiritual power that caused them to tremble or share violently, which they believed would relieve one of sin. The Shakers advocated communal ownership of property, equality of the sexes, and complete celibacy. To achieve this goal of celibacy, the Shakers practiced rigid sexual segregation. Men and women ate at different tables, worked at different jobs, used different staircases to their dormitories, and, of course, slept apart. They were also known for their industriousness, their simple dress, their pacifism, and their creative practicality. The beautiful simplicity of Shaker furniture is highly prized.

The Shaker practice of celibacy made decline inevitable. Without marriages, and thus without children, the sect could survive only by a constant influx of converts, which did not happen.

The Oneida Community

The Oneida Community, a group of Christian Perfectionists, led by the charismatic John Humphrey Noyes, was founded in 1848 at Oneida, NY. Regarded as one of the most successful of America's 40 or so utopian communes, it never had more than 200 participants. The creed was to live without sin, selflessly sharing everything: work, play, intellectual studies. Bible readings, housework, child-rearing and sexual partners.

Monogamous marriage, which might pit a couple's interest against those of the group, was replaced by "complex marriage". All were one family. Children were raised communally apart from their mothers. Sex was also a major activity at Oneida. Noyes encouraged free sex within the community, comparing it to religious ecstasy. Young people were paired sexually with their elders for presumably spiritual benefits. Noyes himself took on the "duty" of initiating virgins, some as young as 13, into "complex marriage".

Later, in 1869, Noyes became interested in eugenics and "scientific breeding" to create a spiritually superior race. Noyes himself sired 9 of the 58 "stirpicults" as he termed the children born of committee-approved parents. The community disbanded in 1881 after the aged Noyes fled to Canada, fearing arrest on adultery and fornification charges.

In addition to sex, hard work was also a major theme at Oneida. The community supported itself by farming, canning fruits and vegetables, and making travel bags, rustic seats, silver spoons, and steel animal traps. The dissolved community's assets were transferred into a private company, that became Oneida Ltd., a leading name in the manufacture of silver flatware.

New Harmony

New Harmony, Indiana, was founded in 1825 by Robert Owen, a wealthy British industrialist. The social and economic reforms Owen had introduced in his British factories for the workers and their families had attracted international attention. He lectured widely in continental Europe on the need for reform, and was moreover willing to devote his wealth and energy to the creation of a new and just society.

Owen's utopian experiment began with the purchase of the Harmony community in Indiana from the Rapines, a religious group that was now moving back to Pennsylvania. Renamed New Harmony, the community consisted originally of 800 recruits and a plan for the construction of a vast communal building, designed for cooperative work and living, but it was never built. Within two years, New Harmony had disintegrated under the stress of bickering, secession, and lawsuits. The failure is traceable to Owen's unrealistic planning. He had advertised for recruits, "industrious and well-disposed", and the response was large and motley. It included radicals, idealists, lazy theorists, free-loaders, and con-artists. Given the diversity of members, a sense of community could not develop. Although New Harmony failed, some of Owen's ideas have had a powerful influence on American social and educational development.

Comment

We have touched very briefly on utopian literature and on utopian communities in 19th century America. The purpose is to determine whether we have guidance here for planning a better social and economic world order. This history of past efforts to design a more equitable society is worth exploring and provides helpful insight, but there is little that we can specifically incorporate into a prescription for Uniworld. These utopian experiments were typically small isolated groups, agrarian, with possibly some small scale manufacturing, and generally held together by a common religious doctrine. Uniworld must be designed for today's world, a world of computers, nuclear bombs, and space ships, and to meet the needs and aspirations of the entire world.

CHAPTER FIVE
UNIWORLD ECONOMIC SYSTEM

Our goal is a an economy that will provide a good standard of living and quality of life for everyone now and for future generations. In the first three chapters we discussed the basic essentials that form the foundation of Uniworld: a world government, a stable world population of two billion, and a protected environment. When this is attained we are more than halfway to our goal even if little is changed in our present economic system. In this chapter we will discuss the Uniworld economic system.

We are primarily concerned about the welfare of our children and grandchildren, but much less so about unborn future generations. We may rationalize that advances in science and technology will provide for these future generations, but this is impossible if we have expended all their environmental capital.

If we are able to provide a good standard of living for everyone now living, we will also be able to pass on a heritage to future generations so that they also can enjoy a good standard of living. A newly-born infant has a life expectancy of about 80 years. To provide a good standard of living for this new-born for the next 80 years requires that we take prompt steps to establish a world government, reduce population to two billion, and protect the environment. If this is not done and the world continues on its present course, this new-born baby, even if living in a favored First World country, will have a rapidly declining standard of living. Only a sustainable economy can protect the welfare of our children and grandchildren and if it is sustainable for 80 years, it can be sustainable for 1,000 years.

Description of Uniworld economic system

In the past few hundred years a variety of economic systems have been tried. The Financial Times of London has offered these definitions of some of the most prominent:

Socialism: You have two cows, and you give one to your neighbor.

Communism: You have two cows, and the government takes both of them and gives you milk.

Fascism: You have two cows, and the government takes both of them and sells you milk.

Capitalism: You have two cows, and you sell one of them and buy a bull.

The Uniworld economic system will be very similar to present day capitalism, a free-market economy with some element of government involvement, but not a planned economy. It will have no resemblance to the disastrous Soviet 5-year plans.

Let's consider a hypothetical primitive tribe, the Yomo tribe, consisting of 100 families. One hundred units of production per day are required to provide the needs of the 100 families. The women take care of the children and the household, and 100 men must turn out the needed production.

However not all 100 men are available for work: 10 men are required for tribal administration; 10 are required for military defense against a hostile neighbor; 10 are disabled or elderly and unable to work.

Only 70 men are therefore available for production, but 10 of these work full time making elaborate costumes for the frequent tribal celebrations, leaving only 60 men available for essential production of basic needs. These 60 men can produce 60 units of production per day, but 10 units of this production per day must be paid to another tribe for a prior debt. This leaves a production of only 50 units a day for the 100 families, far short of what is needed.

To close the gap, the Yomo tribal council decides to eliminate the fancy costumes for the celebrations, and it also makes a peace treaty with the hostile neighbor. This frees up 20 men for essential production, so now the Yomo tribe has a total of 80 men on essential production, with an output of 80 units per day. After deducting the 10 units per day for debt service, the net is 70 units per day for the 100 families, an improvement, but still short of an adequate standard of living.

The Yomo tribal council takes further measures: no new debt is incurred and the old debt is gradually paid off, making 10 more units available; by technological improvements, one worker can now produce

1.3 units per day instead of 1.0 units. Now the 80 workers can produce a total of 104 units per day all of which is available for tribal use, since none is needed for debt service.

Since there is now some surplus available the tribe votes to reassign 3 of the workers back to making fancy costumes for the celebrations. The remaining 77 workers can produce the needed 100 units per day of essential production and the tribe can also enjoy the fancy costumes for the celebration, even though not quite as elaborate as when 10 men worked on the costumes.

The Uniworld economy will be basically similar to that of the Yomo tribe. We will reduce waste; produce basic goods and services with maximum possible efficiency while protecting the environment; and share the output equitably so everyone has an adequate standard of living.

Groundwork

To build an improved economy, Uniworld first must lay the groundwork:

    a. An advanced computer network
    b. A cash-less monetary system
    c. Elimination of government debt

Advanced computer network - Uninet

The Uniworld computer network, which we call Uninet, will simply be an advanced development of our present Internet and other computer networks. An effective Uniworld economy requires access to accurate and timely economic data. Computer capability and power is rapidly improving and if present trends continue for another 10-20 years, the computer networks will make the information age a reality. We do not require revolutionary breakthroughs - though these are very possible. For example, computers at the molecular level have been proposed. But even if we only have improved capability of semi-conductor based computers, this will be sufficient. The term "Uninet" used herein refers to a worldwide computer network, an advanced version of our present Internet.

For example, in Uniworld's cash-less monetary system, every purchase and sale worldwide will be recorded on the Uninet. Let's assume every man, woman, and child in the world - two billion persons - purchased 10 items every day, and that it required l,000 bytes per item to record the transaction in the computer's data base. According to a report in the Washington Post December 1996, the Department of Energy and the Intel Corp have designed a computer that can handle one trillion mathematical operations a second. If such a computer could handle the worldwide purchase transactions, it would take a total of only 20 seconds per day of computer time: 2 billion x 10 x 1,000 / 1 trillion per second = 20 sec

If every person purchased 20 items per day, instead of 10 items, and if it required 10,000 bytes, instead of 1,000 bytes, per item, the computer time would then become 400 seconds, less than 7 minutes. We don't have this capability yet, but it is most likely we will in the next 10-20 years. It is reasonable to expect the exponential increase in the sophistication, capacity, and capability of computers will continue.

Cash-less monetary system

Uniworld's monetary system will not issue any tangible currency or cash. All payments and receipts will be made by electronic transfer on the Uninet. To avoid undue complexity, instead of a single huge computer network, Uniworld will have a network of hundreds of specialized networks, but all coordinated into a master network.

With every sale and every purchase of goods and services executed through the Uninet, Uniworld will have complete and timely information of economic activity and can take prompt steps to correct any major maladjustments. Manufacturers will thus be aware of sales volume and inventories industry-wide and can plan accordingly.

Uniworld will be able to collect sales taxes automatically and immediately. Income tax fraud will be much less feasible, because every transaction is recorded on the Uninet. How the elimination of cash will greatly reduce crime will be discussed in another section.

Elimination of government debt

Uniworld can not afford a universal social security and universal health insurance system unless it can eliminate the cost of military defense and war, and eliminate the heavy burden of payments on prior government debt. With a world government we eliminate the cost of military defense and of war, but how can we eliminate payments on debt?

The present worldwide government debt is enormous. The US debt alone is nearly $5 trillion. Much of the world debt is owed by Third World countries to First World countries. It is unlikely it will ever be repaid, but even if the debt is continually rolled-over, the interest payments alone are in the billions. When the nations of the world merge into Uniworld, a worldwide government, all these debts between nations will be canceled. However this still leaves a huge amount of government debt owed to the private sector - individuals, banks, corporations, and other non-governmental entities. The many debt bonds owed by the different countries to the private sector will be merged into a single Uniworld bond giving appropriate weight to interest rate and quality of risk.

Let's consider several alternatives of what might be done:

Method A: We cancel the debt. Some may say this is simply a debt that we owe to ourselves, so we can just cancel it, but it is not fair. Those that bought government bonds are hurt; those that bought stocks instead of government bonds are unaffected.

Method B: We deliberately cause price level inflation, so the debt can be paid off with cheap dollars. We double wages, prices double, taxable income increases, tax revenue increases, and we use the additional tax revenue over a period of years to pay off government debt. This is not fair. Working people will pay more income tax but they are not hurt because their pay has increased. However the retired and other non-workers on fixed income are hurt by the inflation, by the decline in purchasing power.

Method C: We increase all taxes - sales tax, income tax, inheritance tax. It is fair because everyone suffers more or less in proportion to financial means. The additional tax revenue is used to gradually pay off government debt. However the amount of the debt is so huge, it might take 200-300 years to pay off, unless tax rates are high. For this reason we may also need a tax on net worth of perhaps 1% per year, in addition to the income tax. This tax applies to all assets, not just government bonds, to keep it equitable.

The inheritance tax, above a nominal exempted amount will also be increased substantially. Under current federal tax laws, excess above a $600,000 exemption, is subject to a tax rate starting at 37% and increasing to 55% rate for estates above $3 million. Uniworld may decrease the exempted amount to say $200,000 instead of $600,000, with excess taxed at the current 37%-55% rate. The balance remaining after taxes will then be subject to 2% tax on net worth that applies to all assets.

The high inheritance tax has a value in addition to raising revenue. It prevents the creation of family dynasties of huge wealth that is passed on generation to generation. Even if the total amount is small relative to the size of the economy it creates a perception of a division into haves and have-nots that is best to avoid.

These are high taxes, but this is the fairest way to pay off government debt. We may need to phase in these taxes gradually to give time for the economy to adjust. Once the debt is retired, we will drop back to a more reasonable tax structure, but the high inheritance tax will continue.

Supply

There is nothing profound in the concept of an economic system that will provide a good standard of living for everyone. First we must produce a sufficient supply of basic goods and services and second, we must allocate this supply so that everyone receives a fair share. In this section, we will consider the supply requirement:

a. Produce basic goods and services
b. Regulate business start-ups
c. Produce these goods and services efficiently
d. Produce them in proper quantities
e. Limit production of luxuries
f. Discourage consumerism and advertising

g. Discourage marketing gimmicks

h. Restrict unjustified litigation

Production of basic goods and services

Our basic needs are food, clothing, shelter, and services such as transportation, utilities, health care, and recreation. Most of these can be further subdivided into thousands of specific choices, as governed by supply and demand. There is no need for any government edicts to itemize what should be produced; the operation of a free-market will decide this.

New business start-ups

To maintain a free economy and competition, the economy must not restrict the entry of new businesses into the market place. Detailed information will be available on the Uninet about sales volume, inventory status, and capital investment. Profit reported on income tax returns will be public information, consolidated for an entire industry, though probably not for individual companies. The prospective entrepreneur will analyze this information, aided perhaps by an experienced professional consultant, and decide whether or not to enter the industry.

The new entrepreneur may use his own capital and what he can raise from his family and friends with little restriction. But if he also needs to use "other people's money" there will be some restrictions. He must risk some of his own money, while the money of the outside investors will have a priority position. The entrepreneur may draw a salary, but at a minimum level until the business is profitable. If the business is not successful and is liquidated, the entrepreneur loses his investment first, and the balance, if any, is lost by the outside investors. However if the business is successful, the entrepreneur may then draw a higher salary and will also receive a profit share higher than his investment share due to his increased risk.

Production efficiency

Uniworld will try to eliminate all useless goods and services, and concentrate its resources on useful essential needs. Our next objective is to produce these goods and services with minimum waste and with maximum efficiency.

There is little justification for the multiplicity of package sizes on supermarket shelves. The can of coffee is the same dimensions, and the same price as before, but now it contains 15 ounces instead of 16 ounces. The only purpose is to mislead the public and conceal a price increase. Industry groups will be encouraged to set up standard quality grades and standard sizes of containers. This will simplify consumer choice and bolster fair competition. Non-standard container sizes will be discouraged but will be permitted. They must be prominently marked and will be subject to an extra sales tax.

The metric system will be used worldwide, making price comparisons easier for consumers. Excessive packaging material will be discouraged. Wherever feasible, containers will be re-useable or at least recyclable.

Today the manufacturer of a product such as a washing machine or television set will sell the same basic design under different model numbers to various retail stores. They differ only in minor variations of trim or controls and the only purpose of the different model numbers is to confuse the purchaser and make price comparison difficult. Uniworld will consider this unethical sales practice. If it is basically the same model it must be identified by the same model number.

For mature products that have been made for some years by a number of manufacturers with only minor differences, industry groups will attempt to standardize the design so that all manufacturers are making the identical design. This standardization will provide worthwhile savings in manufacturing costs, in the retailer's cost of carrying an inventory of the complete units and of repair parts.

However Uniworld does not want to discourage innovation and improved designs. The manufacturer is free to develop new designs, but the new design will be subject to a review by the consumer product review board. If, in the opinion of the review board, the proposed design variation is of minor value, it may be made but will be subject to a luxury sales tax. If the design change does have merit, the manufacturer will be encouraged to license it to the other manufacturers so that it can then be incorporated into the standard model.

Production quantity

Under-production and over-production of basic goods and services are inefficient and wasteful and we want to minimize both. Under-production is not merely inconvenient but often leads to costly substitutions. Shortage of an essential raw material leads to plant shut-downs and loss of production. Over-production increases cost of carrying inventories and cost of obsolescence.

The data provided by the Uninet computer data base will minimize both under-production and over-production. The recording of all sales on the Uninet, generated by the cash-less monetary system, will provide valuable guidance to producers in keeping production in balance with demand.

Limits on luxury goods and services

The first priority of the Uniworld economy is the production of the basic goods - food, clothing, and shelter - and the basic services - such as utilities, phone service, education, health care, transportation, government services, and others - in quantity sufficient to provide an adequate standard of living for everyone in the world. All this while protecting the environment for future generations. The second priority is a system that will equitably distribute this production output so that everyone gets his fair share.

Until these basic needs are provided, production of luxuries will be limited. Later on, restrictions on luxuries can probably be somewhat relaxed, but excessive production of luxuries will be restricted as an ongoing policy. It consumes energy and resources and adds to the waste disposal burden.

As in present society, Uniworld will restrict, and in some cases prohibit, the production and sale of harmful products such as cigarettes, alcoholic beverages, narcotic drugs, guns, and others. Uniworld will permit the production and sale of luxury products, but will discourage it by a sales tax. Every consumer product will be classified into one of four groups:

Class A - a basic product
Class B - has some luxury features
Class C - many luxury features
Class D - strictly a luxury

The sales tax will vary with the group, such as:

Class A - 10% sales tax
Class B - 20% sales tax
Class C - 40% sales tax
Class D - 60-100% sales tax

Determination of the group classification will be decided by a panel comprising representatives of the government, industry, and consumer groups.

Products will be divided into broad groups such as television sets, automobiles, mattresses, etc. and each group considered independently. For example, a shoe of basic construction made of durable materials would be Class A; if made of exotic materials it would be Class B or C.

Although luxury products tend to be higher in price than a basic product, price is not always a useful guide. A well-made basic product may cost more but last much longer than a shoddy product selling for a lesser price.

Initially there will be many mis-classifications, but errors will be corrected, and within a few years products will gradually find their proper niche. From then on it will only be necessary to classify new products as they come on the market.

Some recreational facilities and equipment such as swimming pools, large pleasure boats, and private planes are inherently expensive and a Class D rating will add another 60% or more to the cost, making them affordable for very few. These will be purchased by a rental company, or by a community group, rather than by an individual, and the purchase and upkeep cost can be shared.

Consumerism and advertising

America is afflicted with "excess-consumption" disease. We have 5% of the world population, but we consume more than 25% of the Earth's resources. If we do not spend rapidly enough, the economy will slow down, unemployment will increase, tax revenues will fall, and we will have an economic depression. It is un-American to save; it is our patriotic duty to spend and spend. And this huge consumption brings with it the baggage of high environmental costs - increased rate of exhaustion of natural resources, and increased toxic wastes and pollution.

Materialism is not inherent in our nature - all the major religions renounce the evils of excess. Our individual goal is a happy contented life and this can be realized with a basic quantity of food, clothing, and shelter, along with a few modest non-essential luxuries. We do not need a 5,000 square foot home; we do not need a $75,000 car; we do not need 50 pairs of shoes. We can be happy with much less.

The purpose of advertising is to encourage purchases. In America hundreds of millions of dollars are spent each year on advertising, and the total expenditures worldwide are staggering. Proponents of advertising point out it educates the public about new products, and explains the advantage of one product over another. But with no really important meaningful differences between competitive brands, much ado is made of vague meaningless claims. When Budweiser advertises its beer there is little pretense to any claim of superiority of its product over the competition, but it must be acknowledged that its frog commercials are funny.

Advertising does subsidize TV, newspapers, and magazines. Without advertising the viewing public will need to pay the cost of TV service by donations, or by subscription fees, or by higher taxes if government subsidized as in Great Britain. Newspapers and magazines will be considerably more costly. But the advertisers are of course not providing this free service out of the kindness of their heart; we pay for it - it all goes into the price of the product.

The add-on cost of advertising is not inconsequential. According to published reports, cost of advertising in the US was $500 per capita in 1990 and worldwide $250 billion in 1990. The local supermarket charges $2.68 for a 42 oz box of an advertised brand of oatmeal; the identical oatmeal costs just $1.79 under a generic name. This is a 33% upcharge to cover the cost of advertising.

Advertising is sometimes defended as providing product education and information for the consumer. But a much better source of unbiased information for the consumer is a non-profit product research organization such as Consumer Union, publisher of Consumer Reports. It would be desirable to have at least two independent sources of information so a second opinion is available. These information providers will be regulated and licensed by the government to reduce risk of fraud. The information will be accessed on the Uninet. If you are planning to buy a household refrigerator, you can get detailed information about pros and cons and cost of various makes and models. The Uninet will also list stores in your area that sell the particular make and model of interest to you, and the price.

Although usually denied, TV stations, newspapers, and magazines are often reluctant to report news stories that reflect unfavorably on a major advertiser. Without advertising, newspapers and magazines will be half their present size. Fewer trees will be cut down for paper pulp, less energy will be consumed, and less waste will need to be disposed of. Of course in the not too distant future our daily newspaper will be delivered electronically to our computer which we will read on a paper-thin flat-screen viewer.

Advertising is largely an economic waste. Consumer education and unbiased consumer information is far preferable. Consumer education will be an important part of the school curriculum starting at the earliest grade levels and continuing through high school. TV stations, newspapers, and magazines will frequently feature consumer-related programs and reports.

Uniworld will either ban advertising or restrict it by a luxury tax or by making it a non-deductible expense in income tax calculation.

Marketing gimmicks

Coupons and tie-in sales are a waste. Buy Product A and you get

$1.00 off on Product B. The telephone company will give you free airline miles. Join the store's buyer club, accumulate purchase points, and get a free gift. Subscribe to the magazine and you are entered in their $25,000 sweepstake. Open a checking account at the bank and receive a free food blender.

Uniworld will eliminate all these useless promotions and tie-ins. The consumer does not get something for nothing. These sales methods are an added expense to the seller and this expense necessarily is passed on to the consumer. It distorts the operation of the free-market by making price comparisons more difficult for the consumer, not to mention the hours wasted by the consumer reading the literature to understand what the "deal" is all about. Sellers should compete in the market place by offering the lowest possible price, not by setting up smoke screens. These gimmicks will be banned as unfair competition.

Unjustified litigation

The right to sue, to have your day in court, is an important civil right, but unjustified litigation has great economic and emotional cost and must be minimized. Many lawsuits are nothing more than legal harassment and the defendant is often compelled to settle because legal defense is so costly. Some attorneys are the most flagrant abusers of the judicial system. Representing themselves, they actively seek out who they might sue today. Nothing pleases them more than to accidentally slip on an airplane or trip on an escalator.

In Uniworld the judge will have the discretion to decide who must pay costs of suit if the defendant wins. If it appears the suit lacked merit, the judge will make an award to the defendant for costs of defense. Litigants will be encouraged to submit disputes to mediation or binding arbitration, instead of the more costly court process. Arbitration boards will be monitored to ensure they are competent and impartial.

The threat of malpractice suits is a drain on the cost of medical care and forcing many physicians to practice defensive medicine - ordering many more tests than otherwise would be necessary. The threat of litigation also has hampered the development of new contraceptives, medications, and medical devices. Once a product has been approved by the Uniworld Drug Administration, the company is immune from lawsuit. It is possible, however, that even if a product has been thoroughly tested, a few users might be harmed. If so, they are compensated by an industry wide insurance fund, analogous to workmen's compensation. Of course if many users are harmed, or some seriously, the product must be taken off the market. If the company has acted in good faith, it is protected from jury awards of $2,000 for medical treatment, $100,000 for pain and suffering, and $5,000,000 for punitive damages. Without these reforms, the public pays.

Demand

If we are able to produce sufficient quantity of the goods and services that we need, we have the supply. The other half of the supply-demand equation is demand. People need these goods and service and they will buy them if they have sufficient purchasing power. For most of us, purchasing power requires income from employment.

Full employment is no problem - it is easy to provide a job for everyone. Employ half the people to dig holes, and the other half to carefully fill these holes. Or everybody has a job as a security guard - I guard your house and you guard my house.

The deadly earthquake in Kobe, Japan in January 1995 killed over 5,000 persons and caused over $50 billion in property damage. Economic analysts looking for a bright side to this disaster commented that the reconstruction of the houses, roads, and bridges will create many jobs and give a boost to the economy. The quake was of course a natural disaster, but wouldn't it be better to build 100 houses, then tear them down, then rebuild them, then tear them down, etc? We can create thousands of jobs this way, and no one gets hurt.

Useless work accomplishes nothing; we need meaningful work that performs a useful task or service. This creates jobs, and income, and purchasing power, and demand, and avoids waste. With a stable world population of two billion, and modern industrial and agricultural technology, we can readily produce all the goods and services that we need. This gives us the supply, but we also need the demand that will distribute this output of goods and services equitably so everyone has a fair share.

In a small tribal village the available food can be shared directly, but in a world of two billion persons the most practical way of allocating the supply is by the use of money. Money provides purchasing power. We may need shoes, but this is demand only if we have the purchasing power to buy the shoes. If everyone has a sufficient quantity of money, everyone can purchase what is needed. We are of course referring here to money in the generic sense of a medium of exchange. Uniworld's monetary system will be cash-less, as discussed previously.

Social security system

Those that work, employed and self-employed, have purchasing power earned in their work. But there are many that do not work and have no earned income: young children, the sick, the disabled, the retired, parents of young children, and the unemployed. These too require goods and services, but they have no purchasing power unless they receive money from the government or unless they have prior savings.

The non-workers will receive periodic payments from the government social security system. To avoid discouraging saving, the amount received will not be subject to a "means" test. Even though the person may have substantial savings he will nevertheless receive the full standard benefit. The parent (not necessarily the mother - it might be the father) staying at home to care for young children receives a periodic benefit and so do the children.

A schedule of benefit payments might be something like this:

sick and disabled, unable to work	100% benefit
children to age 18	30%
parent at home caring for child under 6	40%
child 6-12	25%
child past 12	none
retired - age 65 - 70	50%
age 70 or more	100%
unemployed	100%

If the economy is functioning effectively the number of unemployed will be relatively small. The 100% benefit payment received by the unemployed will be adequate to provide basic necessities, but will be substantially less than the average earnings of the employed. Since human nature in Uniworld will be the same as now, we don't want to make unemployment too attractive.

The benefits paid to the non-working part of the population will give them sufficient purchasing power to buy the goods and services they need, so both the workers and the non-workers will be provided for. The workers produce the goods and services and everyone, workers and non-workers, receives an adequate share.

These benefit payments are not welfare. The government is the intermediary between the production supply and the distribution demand. The government obtains the funds needed to pay these benefits by tax revenues - primarily income tax, sales tax and inheritance tax. The social security system is primarily a form of government administered insurance. Everyone is also encouraged to supplement the government social security protection by personal savings.

This differs from our present social security system in that Uniworld benefits are paid to all children under age 18 and to one child-care parent. In our present economy only children in welfare-supported families receive government payments. In a sense this tends to subsidize children and may appear to be self-defeating in a Uniworld social order based on a no-growth population. However this policy will not be fully effective until after a stable 2 billion population has been attained. Then a two-child family and some three-child families will be entirely acceptable.

Credit in Uniworld

Debit cards will replace credit cards in Uniworld. Today we make many purchases with a Mastercard or Visa credit card or similar. This is more convenient and faster than writing a check and is more acceptable to the merchant since the credit card company guarantees payment. For some of us, it is a way to postpone payment, sometimes indefinitely. The banks love these people since the banks can then charge 18%-20% interest on the extended payment time.

Debit cards have the same convenience as a credit card but do not permit postponement of payment; the amount of the purchase is deducted immediately from your bank account. In Uniworld if you can't pay for it now, don't buy it until you can. If you want to buy a TV set for $450, the funds must be in your account. If you want to buy a new car for $20,000, you may need to lease the car if you don't have the full purchase price. With few exceptions, the only available consumer credit will be the purchase of a home.

Business credit will be similarly restricted. Purchases of materials and even major equipment must be paid in full when purchased. Industrial equipment wears out or becomes obsolete and must be replaced. For example, a manufacturing plant may have $10,000,000 worth of equipment. Assuming an average life of 10 years, this equipment needs to be replaced every 10 years, but even in the absence of credit, the company does not need to have $10,000,000 of available cash in its bank account. The company sets up a Reserve for Depreciation of $1,000,000 a year, a tax deductible expense. Since the equipment replacement is spread out over the 10 year cycle, rather than all at one time, the company has the necessary funds without the need for credit.

If you want to start a new business, you must risk your own money plus what you might be able to borrow from relatives and friends. If this is not enough, then you must seek equity capital.

For small purchases, the process is streamlined using a so-called "smart-card", a stored-value card, to supplement the debit card. You electronically transfer say $100 from your bank account and load it into your smart card. Each small purchase you make is deducted from your smart card electronically, taking the place of pocket change.

To reduce the risk of fraudulent use of a stolen debit card, a personal identification number (PIN), advanced encryption, or biometric identification will provide security. Ultimately the debit card might be replaced by a computer chip embedded in your body shortly after birth.

In today's economy the focus is on growth and business expansion. Consumers are encouraged to spend, spend, spend to stimulate the economy. Easy credit with "buy now, pay later" is the pied piper. But the credit economy comes with a price - bankruptcies, bad debt losses, interest costs of deferred payments, and the overhead expense of credit granting and collection of receivables. Uniworld is a no-growth economy with a stable population and doesn't need mindless growth. In Uniworld most transactions will be paid for immediately, thus saving the substantial added costs of credit.

Full employment

Today, in the Third World, development is directed toward labor-intensive industries, rather than highly-automated factories, to provide as many jobs as possible. In Uniworld we want efficient production, rather than mere job creation, and we will use the full capability of modern industrial technology, including automation and robotics.

Even though Uniworld will be an extremely stable economy with a highly predictable sales demand, there will be some transitional changes resulting in some unemployment. Unemployed workers receive benefit payments but must be actively seeking employment. They enter in the Uninet their availability for work. Concurrently employers enter in the Uninet their job openings. In this way those seeking jobs can be matched with the job openings.

The government continually monitors the unemployment data. If it appears there is an ongoing shortage of workers, the basic work-week will be increased with a corresponding reduction in hourly rate. If excess number of unemployed the work week will be decreased, with corresponding increase in hourly rate.

This policy is an incentive to improve efficiency. If the desired production output can be made with fewer workers, the work week hours are reduced with no loss of income and with more leisure time. If we have adequate and efficient production output, we can have full employment, shorter work week hours, more leisure time, and still provide support for all the non-working people.

Can we support so many non-workers?

We can't do this if the world population climbs to 10 or 12 billion. We can't do this in a multi-national world that must spend 15% or more of its output for military defense and another 10% for interest on national debt. We can't do this in a world that has exhausted its natural resources and polluted its environment. But in Uniworld we can.

Assume an average life span of 80 years and a stable population. Let's make a rough estimate of the number of non-workers that in effect must be supported by the workers:

children - to age 10	12.50%
children - age 11 to 20	12.50%
parent with young children - call	12.50%
retired - age 65-70	6.25%
retired - age 70-up	12.50%
sick and disabled - call	5.00%
unemployed - call	5.00%
non-workers total	66.25%

This indicates that 33.75% of the population is available for work. With modern industrial technology this 33.75% will easily be enough to provide the basic needs for themselves, for young children, for the retired, for the sick and disabled, and for the unemployed. One hundred and fifty years ago 90% of the population of the United States was engaged in agriculture. Today it is less than 5% and this 5% produces all our food needs with a large surplus available for export.

The workers have income and purchasing power from their work; the non-workers have purchasing power from benefit payments from the universal social security system and from savings.

Why work if income guaranteed?

The sick, disabled, and retired receive benefit payments even though they do not work. There is no "means" test - they receive the payment even though they may have substantial savings and investment income.

If they were required to first exhaust savings to be eligible for benefits, this would be a disincentive to save. In today's world it is almost un-American to save. We encourage people to spend thus stimulating the economy. In Uniworld we want people to save. If you don't need it, don't buy it. If we make and buy what is not needed, it is a waste of time, labor, and resources.

The unemployed are not required to seek work. They may choose to live off savings or become self-employed. However to be eligible for unemployment benefit payment they must be actively seeking work. The names of those receiving unemployment benefits will be a public record on the Uninet and this will discourage cheating. However most will prefer work to unemployment. Unemployment benefits, though adequate for basic living expenses, will be substantially less than the minimum wage.

Labor unions

This is a sensitive issue with no easy resolution. In a free-market economy, we want the factors of production - capital and labor - to compete fairly. The role of government is to set the rules and monitor the rules to insure fair competition, but we want to avoid excess government regulation. If one or two companies dominate an essential industry they have monopoly power and can drive up prices unrestricted by competition. The government rightfully restricts monopolies.

In a free-economy wage rates are set by bargaining between employer and employee, but the employer usually has much greater financial strength. To equalize the playing field, employees therefore have organized unions to increase their bargaining power. The unions have powerful weapons - strike, boycott, and picketing - and the threat of use gives the union strong bargaining power. The large employer with great financial resources also has a powerful bargaining position. If the dispute leads to a protracted strike, the economy suffers.

Union supporters will say this is a price we pay for a free-market economy and to keep the economy in proper balance. But is the outcome necessarily fair? Not every employer is a billion dollar company. A strong union can put a small company out of business. This capital-labor bargaining is not simply a private matter that determines the share of the fruits of the economy that each side gets; it affects everyone else also. A strike by a strong union in a strategic industry, such as public utilities, telephone, mail service, transportation, can cripple the entire economy.

If a union is seeking to correct a low pay scale, its demands are fair, but this is not always the case. Some unions will keep trying to get as much as it can, even if it already has a pay scale far above average. The company of course passes on the higher labor cost by raising the price of its products and everyone else pays.

Uniworld will have a free-market economy, but not laissez-faire; the government will play an important role. We don't want to prohibit labor unions - it is too great an infringement on personal freedom. However we do have now, and will continue to have, laws that restrict the right to strike critical services. The best approach might be to create an economy that is fair, so there is no need for unions.

Labor unions bargain on issues of pay rates, hours, pensions, health insurance, vacations, holidays. In Uniworld most of these will be government mandated and are no longer subjects for bargaining. The universal social security system and health insurance will supersede all employer plans. The number of vacation days and holidays will be standardized worldwide, with flexibility only in choice of specific days. The work week hours will be set by the government, and adjusted up or down periodically to keep employment in balance, as previously discussed.

This leaves only one bargaining issue for the unions, pay rates. The government will of course set a minimum hourly rate, but we will have a range of rates above the minimum, as determined by a free-market economy. If everyone earned exactly the same there would be little incentive to work hard or to innovate. Since there are no company pension plans or health insurance, the employee is not locked into a job by the need to keep these benefits, which makes for a more efficient job market.

A job that has less desirable working conditions will pay more so that it can attract workers. A job that requires more training and greater skills, will have fewer qualified workers available, a lower supply, and will pay more. The free market will prevent wage levels rising excessively. If a particular occupation is in high demand and short supply, wage rates will rise, and this will attract others to get the training so that they too can qualify for this higher paying work. The increased supply will keep a lid on the wage increase. To keep the free-market effective, a union will not be permitted to artificially restrict the supply by limiting union membership.

Labor unions will be permitted, but if Uniworld is successful everyone will receive a fair share, and, in a sense, Uniworld will have preempted the purpose of unions.

Regional differences

Even with a reduced world population of two billion and an advanced Uninet communication system, it will not be feasible to track the economy of the entire world from one central point. Instead, the world will be divided into 10-20 geographical regions, each with its own semi-independent control and management. Each region will keep track of its own production, sales, inventories, and unemployment and make appropriate adjustments. To the extent possible each region will produce its own food, clothing, housing, appliances, and services as needed. There is no efficiency gained by producing the TV sets for the entire world in one factory.

Sales and trade between regions will be unrestricted. The free-market economy will decide when inter-regional trade is appropriate. Some necessary raw materials may not be available in all regions. If the raw material is very bulky and costly to ship, it may be more efficient to process into a concentrate or even a finished product in the region where found, rather than ship the raw material to other regions.

In Uniworld, regions will not compete for new industrial plants; they will locate where it is most efficient In today's economy a half-dozen cities will have a bidding war to induce a manufacturer to build its new plant in their city by offering a free building, tax benefits, and other inducements. Even worse, a city may steal an industrial plant from another city by special subsidies or by promising lower wage rates. Even if the attempt is not successful, the present resident city may be forced (blackmailed in a sense) to provide special inducements to keep the plant. These relocations triggered only by special subsidies rather than economic efficiency is a waste and distortion of a free economy. Uniworld will not permit it.

Even though each region operates semi-independently, it is still one world and one economy. Continual attention will be paid to the economic health of every region - the world must not split into "have" and "have-not" regions, even though there may be temporary short-term differences.

Even though with a small world population most people will be able to live in a good geographic location, some locations will be better than others. One difference will be in the cost of living. If you live in a cold northern area it will cost more to heat your home. You will require warmer clothes so your clothing expense will be higher. If heavy snowfall, cost of snow removal and shorter growing season. Much of your fruits and vegetables will be brought in from warmer areas, and the extra shipping cost will add to your food bill. If less rainfall, more irrigation needed. If you live in the tropic lowlands cost of air conditioning will increase living expense. To equalize the cost of living worldwide, those living in high cost areas will receive a government subsidy, or income tax rebate, or other benefit to compensate for the higher cost of living.

Role of Government

A successful Uniworld requires an effective government - in this case a world government, with of course many functions assigned to regional and local administrative bodies. Today there is a widespread hostility to government, not all of it unjustified. But government is more than a necessary evil. It is an essential player and provides certain necessary services collectively that it would be difficult or even impossible to provide individually. These government services are not free; we pay for them in taxes. But if the government performs these services efficiently and at low cost, we are receiving good value for our "tax dollars at work".

Functions of government

In pure communism the government can own everything, including the clothes on your back, and control everything by edict and regulations. In some primitive nomadic tribal communities, government may be virtually non-existent. In Uniworld the government will have important functions, but these functions will be limited to those that can be performed more effectively by the government than by the private sector. If the private sector can handle the function at a lower cost, it should be allocated to the private sector.

Although many government employees are dedicated and hardworking, many others, protected from risk of discharge by civil service regulations, are otherwise. We do not want government employees subject to whims of politics, but civil service regulations should be made flexible enough to permit the discharge of an obviously poor worker without the necessity of a special act of Congress.

There is no precise dividing line between what should be handled by government and what by the private sector. If the private sector can do it, give it to the private sector. The government should only do what the private sector can't do or should not do. Let's consider a few:

function	gov't	private
universal health care	x	
retirement pensions	x	
social security	x	
unemployment insurance	x	
phone, electric, gas		x
water, waste disposal	x	x
criminal justice system	x	
prison operation	x	x
schools	x	x
public roads	x	
public transportation	x	
libraries	x	x
recreation facilities	x	x

These allocations are not carved in stone. Some trials may indicate that many functions now handled completely by government can be administered by the government but with the operation itself contracted to the private sector. The most suitable are tasks that can be readily defined and overseen.

Uniworld tax system

To perform the functions allocated to the government, it must have sufficient income and this income is generated by taxes. The public almost always feels that taxes are too high, which may or may not be true. Assuming these are all necessary functions, it depends primarily upon how efficiently the government is performing these functions. If performed efficiently the taxes are not too high.

Uniworld will have several kinds of taxes: income tax, sales tax, value-added tax (VAT), inheritance and gift tax. Of course no tariff or import duty revenue since all one world. User fees from some highways, bridges, and recreational facilities will provide additional revenue, but the main source of funds will be taxes.

The primary purpose of taxes is to provide revenue for the government, but the tax structure can also direct social policy. The income tax, and especially the inheritance tax as described in the earlier section relating to payoff of the government debt, will be highly graduated to restrain the gap between the haves and have-nots.

Our current income tax is ridiculously complex requiring thousand of pages of interpretation and providing full employment for CPAs and tax lawyers. Much of tax law is in a gray zone where the outcome is often unpredictable. In Uniworld there will much less of an income gap between the haves and the have-nots and less need for convoluted efforts to level the playing field. The Uniworld income tax will be a graduated tax, simple and clear.

The sales tax will also be a major source of government revenue. This is normally viewed as a regressive tax unfair to those with lower income, since they spend a larger proportion of their income on items subject to the sales tax. However the Uniworld sales tax will be small on most necessities and will apply primarily to luxury goods. The purpose of this structure is to discourage the production and consumption of luxuries.

With today's industrial technology 675 million workers (37.5%) can easily provide the basic essential goods and services for a 2 billion population.

Uniworld tax burden

According to the US Dept. of Commerce, total government expenditures in 1991, federal, state, and local combined, was $2,379 billion. Almost 50% of these expenditures was federal, and the rest was state and local. Some of the major items were:

1991 expenditures		possible saving?
366 billion	- national defense	366 billion
329	- education	88
168	- public welfare	168
66	- highways	40
57	- natural resources	35
43	- postal service	--
39	- health	--
39	- police	20
33	- housing	33
31	- sewage disposal	15
29	- prisons	15
19	- veterans' services	19
247	- interest on debt	247
377	- social security, Medicare	--
76	- gov't employee pensions	35
22	- unemployment compensation	10
438	- misc functions	100

2,379 billion ....Total 1,191 billion

The table above shows the breakdown of the $2,379 billion government expenditures in 1991. The column on the right is a very rough estimate, perhaps somewhat over-optimistic, that $1,191 billion might be saved in Uniworld, a reduction of about 50%.

The largest savings are the expenditures for national defense (a world government, no military forces needed), and for interest on debt (no debt, no interest). Substantial sums will be saved also in expenditures for education, highways, public housing, and waste disposal A stable population that is not growing will require fewer new schools, fewer new highways, fewer new sewer lines, less new public housing. Also less crime, as discussed later, so less money needed for police and prisons.

These savings will make it possible for Uniworld to provide a generous universal social security system and generous universal health insurance.

Tax cheating

The income tax in the United States is a voluntary reporting system. Many report because they fear the consequences of not reporting. Most are willing to pay their fair share, but they may have second thoughts if they think many others are cheating. The IRS might be collecting 90% and missing only 10%, but in their perception, 40% are not paying income tax and getting away with it.

Consequently it is critical that tax cheating be minimized. Much of this tax cheating is found in the underground economy, estimated to be 10-20% of gross national product, most of which is conducted in cash and not reported on a tax return. Uniworld has the solution - the cashless monetary system with all transactions electronically recorded on the Uninet data base.

Other features of Uniworld economy

In this section, we will touch on a number of other ways in which the Uniworld economy differs from today's economy.

Business cycle

The fundamental concept of classical economics is supply and demand. Ask a question relating to the economy, and the answer, often as not, somehow relates to supply and demand. This is often shown in graphical form with price level on the vertical scale and Gross Domestic Product (GDP) on the horizontal scale. The Demand curve slopes downward and the Supply curve slopes upward and where they intersect indicates the presumed equilibrium point of the national economy on that date - the price level and the GDP.

This equilibrium point however may be well below full employment. To stimulate the economy Keynesian economists believe the government should increase government spending and reduce taxes. The monetarist school of economics, chaired by Professor Milton Friedman, wants the government to adjust the money supply, in this case upward. The idea is to shift the demand curve and the equilibrium point to the right and increase employment. However this also moves the equilibrium point higher on the vertical price scale, so now we have inflation. The Federal Reserve Board may also move the interest rate up or down, another way to manipulate the economy.

The Uniworld economy is a free-market profit-motivated economy that will be primarily self-regulating. A key factor in keeping supply and demand in good balance is the computer network and the cash-less economy. Every business transaction, purchase and sale, will be concurrently reported on the Uninet, and inventory calculated for individual companies and for product groups. This information will guide the manufacturer to increase production, decrease it, or continue unchanged, thus avoiding shortages or excess inventories.

With a stable population the needed annual production of basic products can be very accurately estimated - the amount of food needed, clothing, bicycles, homes, washing machines, TV sets, etc. Income and purchasing power will vary very little from year to year, so sales demand will be quite stable and uniform.

The government will not attempt to control prices or establish production quotas. The government will make information available to the manufacturer to guide his planning. If he over-produces the glut on the market may cause prices to drop and he may lose money. If he restricts production, prices may increase, but this will invite new competition into the industry..

The efficient operation of a free-market economy requires competition. Monopoly, domination of an industry by one or two companies will not be permitted. The government will take steps to ensure that enough companies are active in every essential industry for effective competition.

Inflation

Uniworld has a goal of zero inflation. A rising price level helps the debtor at the expense of the creditor since he can pay off the debt with cheaper money. Some economists believe a little inflation is a good thing, but a relatively low inflation rate of just 6% per year will double the cost of living in 12 years. A person retiring at age 65 with an annuity of $40,000 a year, at age 77 will find this $40,000 annuity has the purchasing power of just $20,000.

Inflation greatly complicates the efficient operation of the economy. If we are able to continually and efficiently produce an adequate quantity of basic goods and services, prices will not rise, the cost of living will not increase, and there will be no inflation. If we divert our production capacity to luxuries and non-essentials, or even worse, to coping with an exploding population, to military preparations, to correcting environmental problems that could have been prevented, then inflation is unavoidable.

How about deflation? Over a period of time, production is likely to become more efficient and prices drop, a decline in the cost of living. This increases purchasing power, which will be most evident in the increased purchases of luxury goods. To a moderate degree this is acceptable provided there is no negative impact on a sustainable environment. However Uniworld will limit excessive deflation by a downward adjustment of hours of work. The goal is no inflation, and little or no deflation.

Balance of trade and foreign exchange

In 1944, representatives of 44 nations met in Bretton Woods, New Hampshire to plan the economic structure of the post-war world. World

War II had not yet ended but it was clear the war would soon be over. The goal was to design an economic order of international cooperation and to avoid repeating the events of the 1930s that led to the war. The conference established two important financial institutions: the World Bank and the International Monetary Fund (IMF), and set rules regarding monetary exchange rates and international payments.

Over the period 1879-1934 the gold standard was the international monetary system. Each nation defined its monetary unit in terms of a fixed quantity of gold. A nation's stock of gold determined its money supply. The national currencies of the various countries thus had a fixed relationship to one another. If Country A has a negative balance of trade with Country B, it settles the difference by payment of gold to Country B. Country B now has more gold so its price level rises and its interest rates fall. Country A has less gold so its prices fall and its interest rate increases. The lower prices in Country A induce Country B to buy more from Country A; the higher interest rates in Country B induce Country A to invest more in Country B. So now the gold flows back to Country B.

The gold standard automatically corrects balance of payment deficits or surpluses, but it broke down in the Great Depression of the 1930s. As business activity and employment plunged, each country tried to increase its exports, and avoid a balance of payment deficit and outflow of gold. Each country devalued its currency in terms of gold to make its exports more attractive. The gold standard collapsed and international trade contracted to a trickle with the tariff barriers of protectionism.

At the Bretton Woods conference in 1944 the major countries adopted a monetary system based on gold and the US dollar as international reserves, and semi-adjustable exchange rates. Each member of the IMF was obligated to define its monetary unit in terms of gold or dollars. Deficits were paid by borrowing from the IMF. This system will work successfully if a nation sometimes has a payment deficit and sometimes a surplus, but not if a nation has persistent deficits. Under the Bretton Wood system, the IMF allowed a nation to devalue its currency by 10% to correct a fundamental balance of trade deficit. Greater reductions required approval of IMF Board of Directors, to guard against arbitrary and competitive currency devaluation.

This system worked fairly well but broke down finally due to persistent United States deficits and the drastic decline of American gold reserves. On August 15, 1971, President Nixon suspended the dollar's convertibility into gold, thereby floating the dollar, its value to be determined by market forces.

Since then we have had a loose system of "managed floating exchange rates", with prolonged periods of dangerous misalignment among major currencies, and exchange rate volatility. Bretton Woods has been successful in combating protectionism and encouraging an open world economy. The need for reform is recognized, some advocating even a return to the old gold standard, but there are widely diverse opinions of what should be done.

Fortunately Uniworld need not contend with problems of exchange rates, tariffs, protectionism, and balance of trade. Uniworld has one currency, no exchange rate. and no tariffs. Just as there is no balance of trade problem between Nebraska and Ohio, there is no balance of trade problem among the various regions of Uniworld.

Summary

The Uniworld economy will be vastly superior to our present economy. The world government will avoid the tremendous costs of military defense and of war. Instead of a population growing uncontrollably toward 10 billion and more, Uniworld will have a stable 2 billion population. We won't need to be frantically building more cities, more roads, more schools, more manufacturing plants trying to keep up with an exploding population and a disappearing natural resource base.

The Uniworld economy will use an extensive information data base to guide the world economy and a cash-less monetary system. No longer the heavy burden of interest on public debt. The public debt will have been liquidated and the government budget will operate without a deficit.

Uniworld will concentrate on efficient production of basic goods and services in required quantities, with restrictions on luxuries, consumerism, advertising, marketing gimmicks, and credit.

Because of a stable two billion population, small enough to avoid excessive strain on the environment, the economy will find a stable balance without the peaks and valleys, booms and depressions, inflation and deflation of our current system.

Unemployment will be minimal, limited mostly to temporary transitional changes. Taxes will provide adequate government revenue to permit social security and health insurance for everyone, including the non-working part of the population, without a budget deficit.

The economy of Uniworld is not a brilliant conception of a radically new economy that will transform the world. It is our familiar free-market economy, but designed to reduce waste, encourage efficiency, discourage needless consumption. It is a no-growth economy, but there will be steady gains in standard of living with improvements in technology. The guiding principle is "small is beautiful", to quote E.F.Schumacher. If you don't need it, don't buy it. The cash-less monetary system which records all transactions electronically on the Uninet computer network will help keep the economy on track.

Some of these changes can be made now, but to achieve our goal of a good standard of living for everyone, it must be based on the foundation of a world government, a population limit of two billion, and a protected environment.

CHAPTER SIX
UNIWORLD CITIES

The amenities provided by our homes and our cities greatly affect the quality of life. If poorly designed they will also degrade the economy and our standard of living. This is the subject of this chapter.

City design in Uniworld

Each metropolitan area will be a standard 500,000 population comprising 5 cities of 100,000 each, each about 4 miles in diameter. One city will be at the center, with each of other four cities radiating from it, north, south, east, and west, like spokes on a wheel, about 10 miles from the center city.

If the city group is located along the coast or other waterway, near mountains, or other terrain limitations, the satellite cities will be placed in the most appropriate location, not necessarily due north, south, east, and west, but still about 10 miles from the hub city.

One circular loop highway will be located just outside the perimeter of the hub city. Another loop highway will be located about 8 miles from the hub city, on the near side of the satellite cities. This highway layout of four spokes and two loop roads will provide easy access to each of the five cities. The area between the core city and the satellite cities will be available for an airport, farms, golf courses, and other recreational uses, but most of it will be natural undeveloped land. The overall plan will resemble a tinkertoy construction.

Each of the five cities will have a population of 100,000 and cover an area about 4 miles in diameter, with a population density of about 10,000 per square mile. The commercial area will be in the center of the city, with the residential area surrounding it in an outer ring. Each city will essentially be self-contained, with all the stores, schools, factories, offices, churches, and hospitals in the center, and all the homes and apartments in the outer ring. The residential district will include some playgrounds, community centers, and branch libraries, but all other public areas will be in the central commercial district.

The hub city will be similar to the satellite cities except it will also have the government offices, law courts, major university, and specialized medical facilities for the entire 5-city metropolitan area.

By avoiding urban sprawl, cost of construction for utilities and for roads are greatly reduced. Most persons will live, work, shop, go to school, and play within their own city. If the city is limited in size, and if all non-residential services are concentrated in one central commercial area, travel distance is minimized. We avoid the extra air pollution, waste of energy, and waste of time of traffic congestion if most people can walk or ride a bicycle to work, school, and shopping. It has been estimated that traffic congestion in the Unites States costs $50 billion a year in lost time, extra fuel consumption, and wear and tear on brakes.

In today's world with a near 6 billion world population many people prefer to work at home and avoid the long commute to work. Computers make this feasible for many jobs. Uniworld will not have long commutes - most will live only 10-15 minutes from work - so no special need to work at home. Most of the work-at-home jobs will be held by mothers (or fathers) of pre-school children, so they can combine work with child care.

City location

For maximum efficiency almost everyone will live in cities to avoid the waste of urban sprawl. Since the world population will have been greatly reduced, cities can be located in the most desirable locations taking into account terrain, climate, scenic beauty, proximity to outdoor recreation, and risk of natural disasters. In today's world the most desirable sites for cities have already been settled, so that many of the remaining sites available are marginal - in flood plains, very hot, very cold, mountainous, in area of volcanic or earthquake risk, swampy ground, or otherwise undesirable. If we are forced to locate cities in less desirable sites because nothing else is available, this increases the economic cost and degrades quality of life.

With a world population of two billion, instead of our present near 6 billion (and heading to 12 billion and more) we will be able to locate almost every city in a fairly desirable location. In general the most congenial climate is found in the temperate zone, such as southern California and the north coastal area of the Mediterranean Sea. The Arctic area is cold and the tropics are hot, though some locations in the tropics at high elevations are fairly comfortable. Locations along the coast and near lakes and rivers are often the most attractive.

Avoiding high-risk locations

We must also take note of the risk of natural disasters such as floods, hurricanes, volcanoes, tornadoes, and earthquakes when locating Uniworld cities.

We must not locate cities in flood plains of major rivers such as the Mississippi and we must not rely on dikes to confine the river; the 100-year flood will breach the dike. In Holland, in 1228, 100,000 persons were drowned by sea flood in Friesland. The Huang He River flood in China in 1931 caused the death of 3,700,000 persons. Heavy monsoon rains in Bangladesh, in 1988, inundated three-fourths of the country, leaving 30 million homeless. Cities may be located near major rivers if on high ground, but not in the floodplain.

Hurricanes are huge tropical rainstorms with winds that swirl rapidly around a calm dry central "eye". To be classified as a hurricane wind speed must exceed 74 mph. Typical size is 375 miles in diameter. The coastal areas of southeastern United States are subject to severe hurricane damage. Hurricane Andrew in 1992 was responsible for a loss in excess of 20 billion dollars. In 1970, a hurricane killed over 300,000 persons in the Bay of Bengal, Bangladesh. Much of the damage caused by a hurricane is due to the high winds and heavy rain, but mostly it is the ocean sweeping away oceanfront homes. As the hurricane moves inland, its force diminishes. In Uniworld oceanfront homes will not be permitted unless built at sufficient elevation above sea level to avoid hurricane storm damage.

Volcanoes are openings in the earth crust that emit molten or partly molten rock. A volcano is considered active if it has been active in historic times, but it is not always clear whether a volcano is extinct or merely dormant. Most volcanoes are found where two tectonic plates meet, such as the "ring of fire" around the Pacific Ocean rim. It is estimated there are about 600 active volcanoes around the world, most of these along the Pacific rim.

Usually there will be some preliminary indication of an impending eruption - emission of fumes, lava flow, etc. The lava flow is generally rather slow, but sometimes it is faster than can be outrun. Heat from a volcano can melt glaciers or snowcaps and cause massive mudslides. Destruction from a volcano is usually localized, but a large eruption can blow huge quantities of volcanic ash into the atmosphere. The most lethal effect of a volcano is the Nuee Ardente, a glowing cloud of superheated ash, gas, and solid debris, that kills through both blast and heat.

In AD 79, Vesuvius destroyed the city of Pompeii with ash falls, and Herculaneum with a mudflow. In 1902, a Nuee Ardente flowing down from Mt Pelee on the island of Martinique, killing 30,000 people in the city of St. Pierre.

Volcano risk is fairly predictable and is usually limited to an area close to the volcano. Some volcanoes have been inactive for over 1,000 years, and it may be only a low risk to locate a city close to it, but if there is an equally good site farther away, this would be the prudent choice. In 1991, a 2-day warning that Mt Pinatubo would erupt probably saved 10,000 lives at Clark Air Base and nearby Philippine cities.

Tornadoes are whirling columns of air, reaching down from a cloud during a thunderstorm, with wind speeds up to 300 mph. They are relatively small and short lived, about 500-2,000 feet wide, moving about 28 mph along a path of perhaps 16 miles long, but they can carve a trail of tremendous destruction. In the United States about 750 tornadoes are reported each year, mostly in the Middle West states, but they can happen almost anywhere. There is no way to predict in advance where a tornado will strike, but the Weather Bureau maintains a tornado watch during the tornado season, and issues warnings when a tornado is developing. The best protection for those in the path of a tornado is a tornado cellar, and the next best is an interior hall near the center of the house, but injury or death is still possible.

Earthquakes are caused by the slippage of rock along one side of a fault with respect to rock on the other side of the fault. More than 800,000 earthquakes are registered on seismographs each year, but only a small percentage are large enough to be noticeable. The earthquake that struck the city of Kobe, Japan, on January 17, 1995 killed over 5,000, injured over 35,000, and destroyed nearly 200,000 homes despite superior construction codes. The Pacific Ocean rim "ring of fire" is the area most subject to earthquakes, as well as volcanoes.

An earthquake. even if of large magnitude, may do little damage if in open land, but if in a city, the death toll and property damage can be severe. California has dozens of known faults, but where and when a strong earthquake will occur can not be predicted. Geologic research is underway to learn how to predict an earthquake, but progress will be slow. By means of sensitive sensors it might be possible to forecast a coming earthquake so that people can leave their homes and go to a safe area away from any buildings. But even if the prediction is correct, it probably will not be known whether the quake will occur in 2 hours, or 2 months. Probably the best we can expect is a forecast such as "A 30% chance of a 6.1 earthquake in the NE area of Smith County within 60 days".

The greatest risk in an earthquake is the collapse of homes, especially if masonry construction and a heavy tile roof. Wood frame homes survive an earthquake fairly well. Fires can break out when gas lines are ruptured, and this can cause heavy property damage. It was once thought that steel-frame office buildings were highly resistant to earthquakes, but in the Northridge earthquake of January 17, 1994 many of these buildings developed severe failure of welded joints.

Some of our best city locations are along the Pacific rim and many Uniworld cities will be located there, even though earthquake risk is high. We will of course avoid building near a major known fault, such as the San Andreas fault in California. In areas with high earthquake risk the building code will guide home design to more quake-resistant construction, and no building more than 5 stories high will be permitted. Seismic geologists have forecast a 86% probability that Southern California will have a 7.0 or stronger earthquake within 30 years. If located directly under Los Angeles, the effect would be catastrophic.

To summarize, we can reduce the loss from floods, hurricanes, and volcanoes by prudent regulations, but we can't do as much about tornadoes and earthquakes, and we will continue to have some losses from these natural disasters. The best we can do now is to avoid known high-risk locations, provide early warning, and set up a worldwide natural disaster insurance plan to reimburse disaster victims.

Risk from outer space

There is one other natural disaster, much less likely to happen, but if it did, it could wipe out much of mankind. This is the risk of the Earth being struck by a large meteor or comet. In the prior section we discussed locating cities to minimize the risk of floods, earthquakes and other natural disasters. Not only is no location on Earth free of risk of being struck by a comet or asteroid, every location on Earth is probably at equal risk, so this risk will not influence our choice of city location. But this is the appropriate place to discuss this risk.

If we were able to detect and track a large incoming asteroid that would impact the Earth say 15 days hence, and if we were able to calculate the exact time of impact within a minute or two, we would be able to calculate fairly accurately the place of impact. If the predicted point of impact was near a metropolitan area, all the people in the area could be evacuated to several hundred miles away. Of course if it was a large asteroid, the entire population of the world would be at risk, but it is better to be 200 miles from point of impact, than at ground zero.

Up to 5 million comets may have bombarded the Earth in its first billion years. The comets, maybe 100 billion clustered in the Oort Cloud, about 1.5 light years from the Sun, can sweep in toward the Sun from any angle. Asteroids tend to cluster in a band between Mars and Jupiter. Since 1973, astronomers have identified 200 sizable asteroids or comets, up to 24 miles in diameter, that cross the Earth's orbit, and new ones are being discovered every year.

The extinction of the dinosaurs 65 million years ago is believed to have been caused by the impact of an asteroid or comet just 6 miles wide, that struck the Earth at the Yucatan Peninsula, in Mexico, making a crater 110 miles wide. This area is covered by a large deposit of brimstone, a sulfur bearing rock. The vaporized sulfur, along with the dust and debris from the impact, caused total darkness up to six months. In time the sulfur fumes combined with oxygen and water vapor in the atmosphere, catalyzed by ultraviolet light, forming sulfuric acid clouds, similar to those on Venus. This caused a global winter, lasting anywhere from a decade to a century, dropping worldwide temperature by more than 20 F, cold enough to drop even the tropics to near freezing. The sulfuric acid clouds eventually fell as acid rain, deadly to vegetation.

What is surprising is the effect of an impact with even a relatively small asteroid or comet. The Earth is about 8000 miles in diameter and assume it is hit by an asteroid 4 miles in diameter, and about the same density. The mass of the Earth compared with the asteroid is about one billion to one. The effect of course is magnified by the high speed of impact. But the Earth is not split into fragments or driven out of its orbit, careening off into outer space. The damaging effect of the impact is the effect on global weather, temperature, vegetation, and life forms so dependent on a benign climate.

The risk of collision with a large asteroid or comet is estimated about once in 100 million years; a larger collision that might kill 25% of mankind about once in 500 million years; so this does not appear to be an immediate concern. But this doesn't mean we can forget about it for the next 90 million years - we could be at high risk even now and not know it. The risk is sufficient to justify research to locate and track asteroids and comets that are a possible hazard. An early warning system of small telescopes around the world might cost about $10 million a year, which is only 1/2 cent per capita. With early warning of perhaps 100 years or so, we would have time to plan a space project to nudge the incoming asteroid with a rocket to a slightly different trajectory.

There is the anecdote of the little old lady that was informed of some astronomical catastrophe that might happen in 4 billion years. "Oh dear" she exclaimed. "In only 4 million years!". "Four billion years, not million", she was informed. "Thank God!" she said.

House design

Homes will be of moderate size, typically 1200-1800 square feet, 2 or 3 bedrooms. Some families will have 3 children, but most will have 2 children or fewer. Moveable interior partitions will make it possible to adjust number of bedrooms to suit changing family size. For economy many homes will be row style with common walls. Lot size will be rather small, with yard space enough for a small garden. However small parks will be scattered throughout the residential area to encourage neighbors to get to know each other, rather than every family isolated behind closed walls.

For economy of cost, home design and home construction will be standardized, to a limited number of different designs. Many homes will be constructed of factory made modules assembled at site. We will have a number of different exteriors, so all homes will not look as if stamped out by a cookie cutter, but there is no need for thousands of different designs. Lack of standardization and a multiplicity of styles and designs is wasteful and increases cost. The interior requirements of a family of four is fairly consistent. Moveable partitions will permit a degree of flexibility, and individuality can be expressed by interior decoration treatment, wall color, house plants, and paintings.

Most of the furniture, especially storage items such as bookshelves, cabinets, dressers, bureaus, as well as all the major kitchen appliances, will be built-ins. Beds and tables might also be designed to fold into the wall when not in use. All the basic free-standing furniture, such as tables, chairs, beds, will be included in the price of the house.

At least half of the residences will be apartment rentals, primarily for singles, childless couples, and empty nesters. Most of these will be furnished one bedroom and two bedroom units.

If you are not satisfied with the approved standard designs or if you want a larger home than 1800 square feet, you are free to build what you want, but this will be subject to a luxury tax. A very large home, say 3500 square feet, will have a luxury tax of 100% of cost of home.

Home ownership

In today's world, home ownership is a virtue, like Mom and apple pie, the hallmark of a good citizen. Unlike a tenant, a home owner takes pride in his home and in his neighborhood. He mows his lawn regularly and keeps his home spic and span. It is also a foundation of financial security. As he pays down the mortgage, he is increasing his equity, and in addition the home is increasing in value and he is building a nest-egg for retirement.

Many of these virtues of home ownership will be still valid in Uniworld. Human nature doesn't change, though there can be cultural changes. A tenant can take pride in his home, even if somewhat less so than the owner who has the additional motivation of a financial stake.

However homes in Uniworld will not appreciate in value, since the Uniworld economy strives for a stable, non-inflationary price structure. Savings for retirement do not depend necessarily on investment in a home; there are other forms of savings. But even if a home does not appreciate in value, owning a home can cost less than renting a home, provided the owner is willing and able to handle most of the home maintenance. However renting an apartment is usually less expensive housing than owning a home.

Home ownership has the disadvantage of making it more difficult to move to another city or even to move to another home in the same city. You may change jobs and need to relocate. Because of a change in family status, your home is now too small or too big. You may want to have the experience of living in another part of the world. Your children have moved to another city and you want to live near them. There are substantial expenses and time in selling your home and buying another (broker commission, escrow fees, financing charges, etc), and even if you sell it for the same price you paid for it, it may take 6 months or longer.

If you are renting, you can normally move after giving 30 day notice and your only expense is the cost of moving. Less stuff will need to be moved because many homes and apartments will include furniture, much of the furniture will be built-ins, and the anti-consumerism culture has reduced the amount of possessions you have accumulated.

Transportation

With small compact cities, bicycles and walking will take the place of the private automobile. Elderly and disabled will use small electric battery driven vehicles similar to a golf cart. This will also create a better sense of community. Instead of the anonymity of automobiles, people walking or riding a bicycle frequently over the same route will get to know each other. You may own a private automobile but it will be discouraged by a luxury tax on the car and on the fuel.

Public transportation will be available within the 5-city complex by electric powered trains or trolleys. The power will be fed from a central generating station through rails or overhead wires. These are preferable to fossil-fuel powered buses. Buses have largely replaced electric vehicles in today's world because our cities are constantly growing and bus routes are more flexible for route changes. In Uniworld, the cities are essentially unchanging and stable, so a vehicle, even though confined to rails or overhead wires, is preferable since it does not require fossil fuel.

Electric trains will be used for trips up to several hundred miles. For longer trips, planes will be used, as we do now, but we will need a good energy source to replace fossil fuels.

Living outside of cities

A world population of two billion, as it was in 1930, may seem somewhat sparse compared to our present population of near six billion, but this means 20,000 cities of 100,000 each, grouped into 4,000 metropolitan areas of 500,000 each.

Even though more than 90% will live in these cities, there will be some exceptions. Farms, mines, timberland tracts, commercial fishing areas are not always located immediately adjacent to the city. If distant from the city, those working in that area will live in a nearby small town. They go to their work each day same as if they worked in a factory. The only exception might be owners of small farms who might prefer to live directly on their farm.

City dwellers will of course have the opportunity to get out of the city in their free time. Uniworld will have national parks, campgrounds, vacation resorts same as now. Highway restaurants and motels will be available for travelers.

Still there are many that would prefer to live in a rural area rather than in a city. City high-density dwelling is more efficient than scattered homes and avoids long commutes to work, but some people do not need to commute to work - retired persons, writers, artists, and the increasing number of those that work at home over the computer network. Yet even if they don't need to commute to work, they need to shop, go to the dentist, theirs kids need to go to school. We don't want to have the entire world carved up into 2.5 acre parcels of land. It is more cost effective and less damaging to the environment if everyone lived in the city wherever this is feasible.

However we don't want to prohibit living outside of the city. A compromise is to license the development of a limited number of rural housing tracts located in areas that have minimum adverse impact on the environment. Those persons that feel very strongly about wanting to live out of the city could do so, but the cost of leasing or purchase will be high and subject to a substantial luxury tax.

Inter-region mobility

Most of us live our entire lifetime in one area. Life is an experience and many of us would welcome the experience of living in several different parts of the world and Uniworld will encourage this. Most of the jobs and type of work in one region will also be found in other regions. If you live in an apartment or a rented house, moving will not require selling a house. Houses and apartments will be furnished, so you mustn't move or sell a mountain of furniture. Because of Uniworld's anti-consumerism you haven't accumulated a lot of extra "things".

Even though moving involves a fair amount of cost, which would be avoided if everyone stayed put, Uniworld will encourage some amount of moving between regions. An important element in Uniworld is the blending of diverse groups into a homogeneous society. If no one ever moved, there is the risk of developing regional isolation, regional cultural differences, and possibly even inter-regional hostility. Moving stirs the pot a bit and helps maintain a one-world feeling.

Even though we will equalize cost of living over the entire world, some locations are better than others. We don't want to have every one moving to the French Riviera and yet we don't want to restrict people from living where they wish.

The best solution is the free-market. The most desirable cities will have the highest rents and the highest price for homes. If you want to live there, you may, but it will cost you the most, so you might decide to move to another city, not quite as good as your first choice, but the cost is less.

However in one respect Uniworld somewhat restricts the normal operation of the free market. Today, if there is a large demand for homes and rental units in City A, pushing up prices, investors will be induced to build more homes and apartments to take advantage of the profit opportunity. The increased supply will keep supply and demand in balance and keep a lid on price increases. However Uniworld does not want City A, or any other city, to increase in size beyond 100,000 population, so the increase in supply to meet the increase in demand will not be permitted. The result is that housing costs will stay high in City A.

But City A does not have a monopoly on desirable living. In Uniworld with a 2 billion population, instead of 12 billion, almost every city will be a desirable place to live. Of course there will be differences, and some cities may be better than others, but no city will be so superior that housing costs will rise to an astronomical level because of the great demand and fixed supply. The city that is considered best must still compete with cities that are almost as good, and yet have substantially lower housing cost. Overall in Uniworld the supply of housing will be large enough to meet the demand, and price differences determined by the free market will keep it in balance.

CHAPTER SEVEN
ENERGY, FOOD, AND SCIENCE

Energy

Survival of all life, plant and animal including humankind, depends upon an external supply of energy, the Sun, to provide food. The Sun provides the energy for the growth of plants by the process of photosynthesis and the plants in turn provide the energy for plant-eating animals. Meat-eating animals receive their food energy by eating plant-eating animals lower on the food chain.

Life can not function without energy and modern industrial society is especially dependent on energy. Energy takes many forms: fossil fuels, waterpower, electric power, solar power, tidal power, geothermal, biomass, wind power, etc. Today most of our energy is provided by fossil fuels, but fossil fuels are non-renewable. In the long-run, which is really not long at all, we will depend on renewable sources of energy.

The Sun is the source of almost all power, except tidal power which primarily uses the gravitational attraction of the Moon, and geothermal power which uses the internal heat of the Earth. The Sun, mainly composed of hydrogen, is converting thousands of tons of hydrogen into helium each day by a nuclear reaction, similar to that of the hydrogen bomb, with the release of heat energy. This heat energy is radiated out into space, a small portion of which falls on the Earth, but this is critical to our survival.

In approximately 5 billion years, all the hydrogen of the Sun will have been consumed, and the Sun will die. The dying process of the Sun will extend over 500 million years, passing through the red giant phase, consuming the Earth, and the Sun eventually will end as a small white dwarf. The Earth and all its living creatures will be no more.

Our food supply depends upon the energy of the Sun, directly for growing crops, and indirectly for animal food, which in turn depend on plant food.

Wind power is a form of solar power. The heat energy of the Sun is disbursed non-uniformly throughout the atmosphere, creating winds. If the winds are of sufficient magnitude (between 5-30 miles per hour velocity) they can be used to drive a wind turbine to generate electricity. If the velocity is too high, the turbine must be shut down to avoid damage; if too low, the turbine can not function.

Energy uses and sources

Energy use in the United States is:

residential...17%

commercial...10%

industrial 38%

transportation 35%

Energy in the home is used for heating, lighting, cooking, operation of air conditioners, TVs, and other equipment and appliances. Commercial use is somewhat similar to residential. Industrial use is primarily for operation of manufacturing, farming, mining, and construction equipment. Transportation energy is mostly fuel for automobiles, planes, trains, and ships.

Abundant energy is essential for the efficient functioning of America's industrial economy, but we use far more than our fair share. The average American's energy use is equivalent to the consumption of 5 Mexicans, 12 Chinese, 33 Indians, and 422 Ethiopians. In Uniworld, of course, this disparity will eventually disappear.

Much of the energy for residential, commercial, and industrial use is in the form of electricity. The table below shows how the electricity is generated in California and nationally throughout the country:

	California	U.S.
Coal	13%	54%
Natural gas	46%	10%
Oil	--	6%
Nuclear	21%	20%
Renewables	20%	10%

The 20% California renewables is further divided: geothermal 8%, hydroelectric 5%, biomass 3%, wind 2%, solar 1%, and misc 1%.

Fossil fuels - oil, gas, coal

Fossil fuels primarily are oil, natural gas, and coal, of which oil is the most valuable. Oil is the source of gasoline and jet fuel and the feedstock for the petro-chemical industry for the manufacture of plastics and the thousands of other chemical products. As a fuel for planes, there is no readily available substitute. Modern agriculture depends upon oil to fuel farm equipment and to manufacture fertilizers and pesticides.

Natural gas is an important fuel used primarily in stationery plants, for home heating and cooking, and in electric-generating power plants. To a limited but increasing extent compressed natural gas is used in motor vehicle operation.

Use of coal has increased in many regions following the oil price increase of the 1970s. China, now the world's largest producer, relies heavily on coal to meet its rapidly growing energy needs.

The combustion of all these fossil fuels pumps carbon-dioxide into the atmosphere, along with other pollutants, such as sulfur and nitrogen oxides, carbon monoxide, and hydrocarbons, and is a major cause of global warming, acid rain, and photochemical smog. Transport of oil pollutes the oceans by accidental spills and discharge in normal operations. Coal is the worse pollutant, especially coal with a high sulfur content. Air pollution from coal burning is especially severe in eastern Europe. Strip-mining of surface coal can leave massive scars on the earth, making it more vulnerable to erosion, landslides,. and floods. Acid-drainage from coal mining is a significant source of underground water pollution.

Fossil fuels are the remains of plants and animals that lived millions of years ago. When we burn them we are tapping their biologically stored solar energy. Despite their harm to the environment, fossil fuels still produce more than 90% of the world's commercial energy.

Even if we are indifferent to the environmental damage, the world will need other sources of energy. Fossil fuels are non-renewable; we are mining a valuable resource that sooner or later will be exhausted. The supply of coal is relatively large - enough to last 500 years or longer - but we cannot tolerate the pollution. There are also large deposits of oil shale and tar sands, also unfriendly to the environment, and so far not commercially viable. Forty years ago the remaining supply of oil and natural gas was estimated at about 40 years. Today we are still said to have about a 40 year supply, thanks to more effective technology of exploration and recovery. In recent years many of the new oil discoveries have been made off-shore. Water depth was the main obstacle, limited to about 1000 feet, but in 1994 Shell Oil installed the $1.2 billion Auger platform in 2,850 feet deep water. In 1996, Auger's eight wells produced more oil than the entire nation of Chile. Shell is planning a well in 4000-foot waters for 1998.

It is unfortunate that we have the improved technology to locate and recover oil. It is a valuable resource that will be difficult to replace, especially as a feed-stock in production of chemicals. To simply burn it as a fuel is a tragic waste. The only fuel use that possibly is justified is for aviation fuel; we should use other fuels for automobiles and ground-based engines.

We should conserve the remaining stock of oil and natural gas and the best place to conserve it is to let it remain underground where it now is. But this will not happen; at the present low price for oil and natural gas, substitute fuels are much more costly. For many of the oil-producing countries - Nigeria, Ethiopia, Libya, Iran, Saudi Arabia, Venezuela, etc - revenue from the sale of oil is the principal foundation of their economy. Only a world government, Uniworld, would be able to preserve the remaining supply of oil and natural gas, but the supply will be exhausted long before a world government is in place.

Nuclear Power

The development of nuclear energy as a power source was initially hailed as a great boon to mankind - a peacetime application of the wartime research that developed the atomic bomb. Here was an apparently limitless source of low-cost, safe, and non-polluting energy, but alas, reality set in. The accidents at Three Mile Island and at Chernobyl showed generating plants were far from foolproof. It was not low-cost energy - in the United States, recently-built nuclear plants generate power at a cost of over 13 cents a kilowatt hour, twice the prevailing cost for conventional-fueled plants.

Although nuclear power plants themselves produce no greenhouse gases, the energy used to mine and prepare the uranium fuel does release substantial amounts of carbon dioxide. Worse yet is the problem of decommissioning a nuclear power plant with its highly radioactive reactors and other components after about 30 years of operation. Cost estimates range up to $3 billion per plant.

And worst of all is the safe disposal of nuclear waste - from highly toxic liquid waste that will remain radioactive for thousands of years to hundreds of millions of tons of low-level tailings from uranium mining and processing. Some reactor byproducts have half-lives five times as long as all of recorded history. Billions of dollars have been spent to find a method of safely treating and disposing of nuclear waste but there is still no good solution. It is like the indestructible monster in the horror movie that can't be stopped by fire or bombs. For radioactive waste the only weapon is time; after sufficient time, which may be 10,000 years, the radioactivity is at last exhausted. One current proposal is to consolidate the material into cylindrical shape, encapsulate the cylinder with a glass-type coating, and bury the cylinders in deep shafts in the Mojave Desert. Critics are concerned that during the thousands of years until the material is rendered harmless, earth movements will fracture the cylinders and radioactive waste will contaminate underground aquifers.

Biomass energy

Biomass energy is the chemical energy stored in green plants, from the energy of sunlight by the process of photosynthesis. Trees of many types provide fuelwood, an essential source of energy in the Third World, as well as many agricultural crops and crop residues from sugar cane, corn, and others. Many of these plants grow on land unsuitable for agriculture. Even crops grown for food often leave residues outweighing the edible part of the crop. This residue can be burned as a fuel or converted into chemicals such as ethanol and methanol. If the biomass material is fermented in a digester or biogas generator, it will produce useable fuel gas, and also leave a residue rich in nutrients and organic material that can be used as a fertilizer.

Biomass provides 15% of all energy consumed worldwide and over 90% in some developing countries. In Brazil, ethyl alcohol from the fermentation of sugar cane provides about 50% of the country's automotive fuel. Pulp and paper companies in the United States obtain 55% of their energy needs from wood and other biomass sources.

But biomass as an energy source is not free of problems in the Third World. Excessive use of dung and crop residues for fuel, instead of for soil enrichment, has reduced grain yields. As population has soared, excessive cutting of trees for cooking fuel, has created severe shortages. Around some Third World cities, a wide swath of land has been completely stripped of trees. A typical family might spend 20-40% of its income on fuelwood products, and in rural area, where wood is "free", people are forced to spend increasing time to gather it. In the African Sahel and in the Himalayas, women and children labor up to 300 days a year collecting fuelwood.

Tree-planting programs are essential to solving the fuelwood crisis and also to provide feedstock for alcohol fuel. By absorbing carbon dioxide, trees slow the pace of global warming. By blocking the summer sun, trees reduce consumption of electricity for air-conditioning. Agroforestry, combining tree planting with traditional agriculture, protects crops from excessive sun, wind, and soil erosion, and improves water retention. Certain trees can improve crop productivity by adding nitrogen to the soil while regular pruning can provide substantial amounts of fuelwood.

Windpower

For centuries, rural windmills have collected energy. Windmills were first used in 7th-century Persia and no landscape of Holland is complete without windmills, but in recent times windmills have been replaced by more efficient energy converters. Now windpower, in the form of wind turbines for the generation of electricity, is once again drawing attention.

Air-foil type blades are mounted on tall steel towers. Wind flowing past the blades causes them to rotate, turning a shaft that drives an electric generator, while a transmission in the shaft assembly maintains a constant-speed rotation. The turbine assembly pivots to keep facing the wind as it changes direction. If the wind speed is excessive the turbine shuts down to avoid damage. Underground wires conduct the generated electricity to transmission lines.

Much of the technology was developed in Denmark, and the largest arrays of wind generators are now found in Denmark and in the United States, especially California, which together account for 90% of installed wind turbines. Successful operation requires a location with a dependable amount of wind, found primarily in a mountain pass. In California, the principal wind farms are located at San Gorgonio Pass near Palm Springs, at Tehachapi Pass north of Los Angeles, and Altamont Pass east of San Francisco Bay.

Wind turbines are a supplemental source of generation of electricity, not a primary source, since the wind does not always blow when you need it. Winds are most dependable in winter and spring, and much less so in other months. Operating costs of a wind turbine are minimal - the wind is free - but the capital cost of a single unit can be $200,000 and more. This is renewable energy, and except for some noise, wind turbines are non-polluting. They now account for less than 2% of generated electric power in the United States, but in the future this could become 10%.

Waterpower

Waterpower, in the form of waterwheels, has been used as a source of mechanical energy for many centuries, driving millstones and lifting water for irrigation. Since the early 1900s many large dams have been built to generate electricity. The flow of water released from the dam has high energy due to the difference in elevation, drives against the blades of a water turbine causing its vertical shaft to rotate at high speed. Mounted higher on this rotating shaft is an electric generator which feeds electricity into transmission lines.

Instead of a dam to create the difference in elevation of water level, nature may provide it in the form of a waterfall, such as Niagara Falls, a major hydroelectric facility. However the world does not provide a great number of suitable waterfalls, so most hydroelectric power requires man-made dams.

Unlike wind turbines, hydroelectric power using dams can be a primary power source. The dam impounds a large volume of water sufficient to provide year-round operation even if water inlet flow and rainfall is highly seasonal. Similar to wind turbines, operating costs are minimal, but capital investment is high.

Waterpower is renewable, does not pollute the air or add to global warming, but it does have some environmental disadvantages. The upstream lake created by the dam might flood over much productive farm land and scenic river canyons, and displace many families from their homes. River silt piles up against the dam and prevents it reaching and enriching downstream floodplains. And this same silt reduces the flow of water through the turbines and the amount of electricity generated, reduces the depth of the upstream lake, and eventually the dam becomes useless.

Ocean Energy

Efforts have been made to generate power from ocean waves, from ocean temperature differences, and from ocean tides, with little if any success. Ocean thermal energy conversion, using tropical sea water as a vast solar collector, works like an air conditioner in reverse. Instead of using electrical energy to create a temperature difference, the temperature difference between the ocean's warm surface water and the cooler deep water is used to generate electricity.

Tidal power, which relates to the gravitational attraction of the Moon, (and of the Sun to a lesser extent), rather than the heat of the Sun, is possibly feasible where there are large tide changes, such as the Bay of Fundy in Nova Scotia with a range of 41 feet. In most other coastal areas, the tide range is much less - in New York City 5 feet, New Orleans one foot.

Ocean energy is renewable and non-polluting, but is unlikely to be a major source of energy.

Geothermal Energy

This source of energy taps the internal heat of the Earth, rather than energy from the Sun. In some parts of the world, naturally occurring hot water reservoirs are close to the Earth's surface and can be tapped for generation of electricity or used locally for heating buildings and for low temperature industrial applications. The largest installation in the United States is The Geysers in California. Although the Earth has a vast supply of geothermal energy, this is not a long-term renewable source of energy, since the limited number of feasible sites soon become depleted. Also geothermal energy has some negative environmental effects. The water from some geothermal reservoirs contains harmful salts and minerals and geothermal plants can release undesirable hydrogen sulfide into the atmosphere. Geothermal energy may be a useful interim source of energy, but not a major long term source.

Solar Thermal Energy

Almost all our energy is solar, except nuclear, geothermal, and tidal energy. Fossil fuels are the end products of ancient plants whose growth was dependent on the Sun, as is biomass. Windpower and waterpower, as discussed earlier, also utilize solar thermal energy conversion.

Solar water heating for domestic hot water is widely used in warmer climates. It has declined in importance currently in the U.S. with lower oil and gas prices and elimination of tax credits, but will once again become important as reserves of gas and oil diminish and gas and oil prices increase.

Some experimentation has been done with solar ponds filled with salt and water. The denser salt water on the bottom absorbs heat while the surface water traps it.

More complex systems now in use generate electricity by using reflectors, parabolic-shaped mirrors, and lenses to concentrate the sun's rays on to pipes carrying a synthetic oil-based heat-transfer fluid, heating the liquid up to 400 degrees Celsius or higher. The hot liquid produces steam which drives a turbine-generator to produce electricity. However these plants are not currently competitive with plants using fossil fuels at current prices for fossil fuels.

Solar Photovoltaic Energy

This process converts sunlight directly into electricity, rather than the more conventional approach of solar thermal energy. This requires no moving parts and no heat, and only enough light to displace electrons from their orbits in a semi-conductor material and produce an electric current. Photovoltaic energy is the most environmental friendly source of energy, and is the only electric generating technology that does not use mechanical energy or heat energy to turn a generator.

Various kinds of photovoltaic cells have been developed, mostly based on silicon, but some using cadmium telluride, gallium arsenide, gallium antinomide, and other semi-conductor materials. Some use polycrystal silicon, some silicon beads, some thin films of amorphous silicon. It has been proposed that conversion efficiency might be improved by Fresnel lenses to concentrate the sunlight.

At present photovoltaic power costs in excess of 15 cents per kilowatt hour, as compared with 5 cents for natural gas, and 7 cents for nuclear power. With more research, conversion efficiency, now about 15%, will improve. New designs will reduce manufacturing cost, which will be further reduced by economy of scale with volume production. It is likely that in 10-20 years photovoltaic solar energy will be price competitive with fossil fuels and nuclear fuel. Some believe it is price competitive now, if the environmental costs of fossil and nuclear fuels are taken into consideration.

At present photovoltaic power is primarily used in rural areas, distant from any existing power grid. For home use, a roof-mounted solar panel generates electricity during the day and is stored in batteries. When electricity is needed, the 12-volt battery power can be used directly in lights or household appliances, or first converted by an inverter into standard

110 volt, 60 cycle power.

The major future use for solar photovoltaic generation of electricity is to replace fossil fuel plants. Solar power has one serious weakness - it works only when the sun shines, unlike most other energy sources that can operate any time of day or night. Wind turbines have a similar weakness - they work only when the wind blows. One temporary solution is dual generating plants - solar plants that operate during the day, and fossil fuel or nuclear plants that operate only at night. After fossil fuel is exhausted, we can use biomass fuel instead.

Another solution is a world-wide power grid that would provide power from daylight areas to areas on the nighttime side of the earth. This would be feasible only if power could be transmitted long distances with minimum power loss. Superconductivity is now possible only at temperatures close to absolute zero. We will need superconductivity at normal outdoor temperature range, but there is no certainty this will ever be possible.

An article in the October 1997 issue of Technology Review proposed a series of low earth orbiting satellites, at an altitude of a few hundred miles, each with a large inflatable solar power collector, that would power an onboard microwave generator, and beam the power to ground-based rectifying antennas. Sophisticated computer controls, and phased arrays electronic systems would be needed to properly aim the microwave beam. To reduce cost, these same satellites would be used for communication.

A less complex solution is to supplement the solar power facility with two large water reservoirs at different elevations. During the day, the surplus solar power will pump the water from the lower reservoir into the upper reservoir. During the night, water will flow back from the upper reservoir into the lower reservoir, passing through a turbine and driving an electric generator. An alternative to the reservoirs is to use the surplus daytime solar power to hydrolyze water into hydrogen and oxygen. At night the hydrogen is burned driving a turbine generator.

Automotive Fuel

There are several possible alternates to oil-derived gasoline as an automotive fuel. Methanol, or wood alcohol, can be derived from any carbon feedstock, including coal, gas, and wood. Gas is non-renewable; coal is non-renewable and polluting. Although methanol has only about half the energy value of gasoline, it can serve as an efficient clean-burning fuel.

Ethanol, or grain alcohol, is produced by fermenting grain, usually corn, or other biomass feedstock, even municipal solid waste. When produced from tree plantations, the use of alcohol fuels may cause no net increase in atmospheric CO_2, since biomass absorbs CO_2. In Brazil, ethanol from sugar cane provides almost 50% of its automotive fuel.

Electric cars have been around for almost 100 years, but were soon superseded by gasoline-driven vehicles. Once again, electric-driven cars are receiving more attention. Electric motors are simpler than gasoline engines and require less maintenance and electric power is cheaper per mile than gasoline. An electric car emits no tailpipe pollutants and utility power generation produces fewer pollutants than gasoline vehicles.

The major limitations of electric cars are the storage batteries and the limited driving range. The batteries are heavy and costly and must be replaced every few years and yet provide a driving range of only about 75 miles before recharging is necessary. This may be adequate for local use and short trips, but not for a trip of even a modest distance. With a gasoline vehicle you can refuel in a few minutes, but to recharge the batteries of an electric vehicle will require at least several hours. Considerable research is underway to improve efficiency, capacity, cost, and range of storage batteries, but there is no assurance that substantial improvement will be realized. Storage batteries have been around over 100 years; it's a mature technology, not an infant science like computer chips or photovoltaic cells.

Another possible power source for automobiles is a hydrogen fuel cell. Hydrogen enters one side of the fuel cell which is composed of a series of stacked platinum plates. The hydrogen binds to the platinum, stripping off an electron. The electrons are channeled to an electric motor, providing the current to drive the vehicle. The electrons are then returned to the positive side of the platinum plates where they combine with oxygen to form water, the end product.

However hydrogen has two problems; safe storage and energy density. The hydrogen can be stored in three ways: as a compressed gas in a high-pressure tank: by liquefying it and storing it in a high-pressure tank at a very low temperature; by storing it combined with a metal hydride in a special tank. The metal hydride is a material such as titanium-iron or magnesium-nickel that has a strong affinity for hydrogen. Each of these is costly and of limited capacity, though the metal hydride method is probably the safest. A 800-pound metal hydride tank can only store the equivalent energy of four gallons of gasoline.

A proposed modification of the hydrogen fuel cell that might solve the hydrogen storage problem is the direct-methanol fuel cell. It starts with methanol instead of stored hydrogen. Liquid methanol is sprayed into an on-board "methanol reformer", consisting of a cylinder packed with a common catalyst. The methanol is mixed with oxygen from the air, releasing the hydrogen bound up in the methanol. The hydrogen-rich mixture of gases is then injected into a fuel cell, generating an electric current that powers the electric motors of the vehicle.

The automobile of the future will probably be based on a fuel cell or a hybrid combining solar photovoltaic power and a fuel cell.

Aviation fuel

Fuel for aviation and the required auxiliary equipment must have high energy density in relation to weight. Storage batteries are far too heavy. The direct methanol fuel cell described in the prior section might be more feasible than a hydrogen fuel cell. Solar photovoltaic cells can not be the primary power source but might be part of a hybrid.

A high-speed flywheel, spinning up to 55,000 revolutions per minute, and encased in a vacuum housing, might be a supplemental power source to provide the extra power needed for take-off. The energy needed to bring the flywheel up to speed will be provided by ground-based fuel or electric power before take-off.

Until the necessary technology has been developed to power airplanes efficiently and economically using renewable fuel, we should not use fossil fuels for ground based vehicles. Our remaining supply of oil and gas should be reserved primarily as a chemical feed stock, and temporarily only for aviation.

Batteries

To round out our discussion of energy sources, we will mention batteries. Batteries convert chemical energy into electricity. Most batteries, especially the small ones, are discarded once their chemical energy has been expended, but some batteries, such as automobile storage batteries, can be recharged.

The primary feature of batteries is portability. An electric drill must be plugged into an electric outlet for its power, but some of the smaller size drills can be battery driven and not need a power cord.

Batteries are not a source of energy. More energy is expended to manufacture a non-rechargeable battery than the completed battery provides. A rechargeable battery is primarily a device to transfer chemical energy into electric energy. In recharging, electric energy from a primary energy source, is converted back into chemical energy.

Food

From the time of the first Man over one million years ago, he was a hunter-gatherer of food. He hunted animals and collected plant material that was suitable for food. The game animals typically migrated and the suitable plant material in one area might be available in only certain seasons, so Early Man was nomadic, moving from place to place to follow the food supply.

It was only in relatively recent times, perhaps 10,000 years ago, in an effort to better control his food supply, that Man started to plant crops and domesticate animals.

The coming food crisis

All through the ages, the principal work of humans was directed toward providing food. In the Middle Ages almost everyone was involved with farming and agriculture, and even today in much of the Third World, farming, fishing, and the care of livestock is the principal occupation. Despite this, hunger, malnutrition, and starvation has been a continual problem all through the ages.

The "Green Revolution" of the 1960's with its high-tech agricultural methods greatly increased crop yields, making substantial inroads against world hunger, but the "victory" will be short-lived. The green revolution relies on heavy use of pesticides, fertilizers, and fossil-fuel driven machinery, bringing with it severe environmental damage, topsoil erosion, salinization, desertification, water pollution, depletion of ground-water aquifers.

There are two ways to increase total crop output to keep up with the increased demand due to population growth - increase the amount of cultivated land and increase the yield per acre. Only a small portion of the Earth's land area is suitable for farmland and yield can only be increased so far before negative side affects offset any further gain.

Gary Gardner writing in State of the World 1997 describes the problem faced by the city-state of Sumer 4,400 years ago. Their farmland was gradually accumulating salt due to evaporating irrigation water and the crop yield was dwindling. Previously they had responded to the diminished yield by cultivating new land, but now they had reached the limit of land expansion. Over the next 300 years, the accumulating salt reduced crop yields more than 40%. By 1800 BC the combination of a growing population and a reduced food supply led to the collapse of the once glorious Sumerian city-state.

Food production is no longer increasing worldwide. Grain harvest is down 8% in 8 years, meat production is down 1% in 2 years, fish catch is down 7% in 3 years, while at the same time world population is continuing to grow explosively.

Only 10% of the Earth's surface, after subtracting oceans, lakes, mountains, deserts, arctic regions, is suitable for growing food, and much of that 10% is only marginally fertile. Every year much of this precious 10% is being destroyed by urbanization, erosion, desertification, and over-grazing. California's Central Valley is the world's richest farm belt, providing 25% of America's table food. At the same time this area is a fast growing urban area. Each year urban sprawl is gobbling up 20,000 acres of this prime agricultural land.

About 99% of Egypt's 58 million people live in the rich agricultural land along the Nile, comprising only 4% of the country area. In an effort to solve the problem of urban over-population, unemployment, and overworked agricultural land, the government is subsidizing the farming of desert land with limited success.

Fertility of soil is in the few inches of topsoil. It takes 250 to 1,000 years to generate 1" of topsoil, but each year billions of tons of topsoil are eroded away due to ill-conceived agricultural methods. Overgrazing in the Sahara due to population growth has turned vast areas of marginal rangeland into desert. It is estimated that 25,000 square miles of the word's arable land is turned into desert each year because of misuse.

When tropical rain forests are cleared away for agriculture, the nutrients are cleared away with the trees. The nutrients in tropical rain forests are in the trees themselves, with very little in the soil. The farmland so created can be cultivated for only a few years.

According to the FAO (Food and Agricultural Organization) about 800 million of the world population is undernourished. The bulk of this underfed population - defined as less than 2,100 calories a day - is concentrated in sub-Saharan Africa, Haiti, Afghanistan, and parts of Central and South America. Every day about 40,000 children die from starvation and related diseases.

The world grain harvest in 1995 was the lowest in seven years, and the present grain reserve is at an all-time low. We are harvesting less cropland, and this reduced acreage is no longer responding as well to irrigation and fertilization, so yields per acre are now decreasing. The sea is faring no better. All 17 of the world's major fisheries are being fished at or beyond capacity.

In two recent books, Who Will Feed China? and Tough Choices, Lester Brown of the Worldwatch Institute has alerted us to the coming food crisis. With an economy that has grown 50% in the past 5 years, China is eating higher on the food chain - eggs, meat, beer, etc

- and more food per capita. At the same time cropland is being paved over for roads, parking lots, and housing developments while the population is increasing by 12 million a year. Some 3 billion persons live in the rapidly industrializing region in Asia stretching from Pakistan to China and Japan. With the rapid rise in affluence, these 3 billion people will move up on the food chain, and soon the demand for foodgrains will outrun the capacity of the grain exporting countries. The result will be a large increase in the price of foodgrains, and the hardship will be borne most of all by the poor countries of the Third World. Twenty years ago Africa was self-supporting in food and a substantial exporter of food. Now Africa needs to import food to survive.

From 1950 to 1987 the world fish catch more than quadrupled, from 22 million tons to 92 million tons. To protect local fisherman from foreign competition the United States, in 1976, extended its jurisdiction over coastal waters to 200 miles and other countries followed suit. This led to the development of high-tech factory ships that can operate far beyond the 200 mile limit. In the late eighties, more than 700 Japanese, South Korean, and Taiwanese fishing vessels, equipped with 20-40 mile long drift nets, swept an area in the North Pacific the size of Ohio each night.

Over one billion people in the developing countries rely on fish as a major source of protein. Many species including the Peruvian anchovy, the Alaska king crab, North Atlantic cod and haddock, and Atlantic herring, have been over-fished to the point of collapse. And while yields are decreasing, the gross registered tonnage of the world's fishing fleet doubled from 1970 to 1992. It's simply a matter of too many boats chasing too few fish.

The availability of adequate supply of water for agriculture is becoming critical. According to a recent World Bank study, 80 countries, with 40% of the world population, are already suffering from a water shortage. The cause is world population growth which increases the demand for food and irrigation. To make matters worse, much of the water supply is contaminated by domestic and industrial waste, agricultural chemicals, and mismanaged land use. If the drain on water continues at its present pace, the supply per capita will fall from 3,430 cubic meters in 1960 to 667 cubic meters in 2025, an 80% drop within one lifetime.

Underground aquifers of water in many areas are being depleted much faster than they can be replenished by rainfall. Irrigation water often carries a heavy component of dissolved minerals. Evaporation of the water leaves a salt and mineral deposit that accumulates in the soil, eventually making it unfit for agriculture.

While population growth is putting increasing pressure on our food supply resources, international politics adds to the problem. The Western World while providing famine relief to certain Third World countries undermine their own efforts by simultaneously supporting the arms trade. Conflict and war is a primary cause of famine. In some cases famine is even tolerated, if not encouraged as a weapon of war. In Sudan, the population was literally starved out of the central region to give exploiters access to the oil-rich area.

Uniworld Food Supply

Our impending food crisis is caused primarily by our increasing population - now nearing 6 billion and heading toward 12 billion and more. We can not supply adequate food for this many people on a sustainable basis. But Uniworld with a world population of two billion can. Even so, Uniworld will need to manage its food producing resources efficiently and prudently.

With a small population and the requirement for a moderate quantity of food, we will farm the most suitable areas, with good topsoil, good rainfall, and favorable weather during the growing season. We will avoid steep slopes that will be vulnerable to serious erosion. These suitable areas will be large enough that we only need to use part of it, while the rest lies fallow, to be used later while the original cropland in turn lies fallow and given time to recover.

Most of the cropland in Uniworld will use rainfall as its principal water supply, though some might require supplemental irrigation.

Irrigation water often carries with it undesirable dissolved minerals that may end up deposited in the soil and degrade soil fertility.

Uniworld will limit the use of chemical fertilizers and instead use nitrogen-fixing legumes and clover, and crop rotation. Chemicals from fertilizers destroy the natural balance of the soil and run-off pollutes streams and rivers. Since less than half of the fertilizer and irrigation water reaches the crop, drip irrigation, with dissolved nutrients applied directly to the roots of individual plants, are more efficient.

Often less than 0.1% of the pesticide use actually reaches its target and much of the rest may contaminate the soil and water supply. Instead of chemical pesticides and herbicides, Uniworld will use the concept of integrated pest management (IPM) and organic farming. This relies on biological controls such as natural predators, changes in planting patterns, and development of pest-resistant varieties. When pesticides are first used, crop yields may increase temporarily, but later may decline, since the pesticide kills not only the target pest but also its natural enemies. With continuous use of a pesticide, the pest becomes resistant by natural selection. By 1980 more than 400 arthropods (insects, ticks, and mites) as well as 100 plant pathogens (bacteria and viruses) had developed resistance to pesticides. IPM does not try to eliminate pests, but rather to prevent them from causing serious economic loss.

Non-chemical methods, rather than herbicides, can be used to control weeds. Inter-cropping, growing a legume between rows of wheat, can suppress weeds and add nitrogen to the soil. Cover crops that release natural toxins can be effective in inhibiting weed growth, as well as mulches and certain crop residues.

Uniworld will discourage the excessive consumption of meat from grain-fed animals. Grains, cereals, and other plants are a much more efficient source of food for human consumption than meat. Grain-fed beef is especially inefficient, requiring about 16 pounds of grains and soybeans to produce one pound of beef. A pound of poultry or eggs requires 3 to 4 pounds of grain and soy. US livestock are fed enough grain and soy to support five times the country's human population. To produce a pound of beef requires 100 times as much water as to grow a pound of wheat, and 30 times as much energy. More than half the water consumed in the United States is used to grow feed for livestock.

Livestock raised on rangeland, if well-managed, is less objectionable. However some rangelands are over-grazed. As vegetation becomes sparse and topsoil is disturbed, grazing land becomes vulnerable to water erosion in wet areas, and to wind erosion in dry areas. Livestock waste contains nitrates, a significant source of contamination of groundwater and surface water. US livestock is responsible for twice as much organic water pollutants as is industry.

Fish will be a major food source in Uniworld. With a world government that can effectively regulate the fish harvest, and a small stable world population, large quantities of fish can be brought to market at a sustainable level. This is a food source that goes back to the hunter-gatherer stage of early Man, requiring a minimum of human intervention. It is a bounty of nature, there for the taking, providing we use it wisely, and do not poison its habitat.

To prevent the capture of fish too small for commercial use, fishing nets will have a minimum mesh size. Biodegradable nets and other fishing gear will reduce the accidental trapping and death of marine mammals. To some extent fish farming and other aqua-culture methods will be used to raise shrimp and other special varieties of seafood.

Uniworld will encourage biotechnology research to improve agricultural productivity by conventional plant breeding, genetic engineering of plants, biological fixation of nitrogen, and increased photosynthetic efficiency. New crop varieties will be developed that mature early, that are pest-resistant, and can tolerate very acid soils, high salt content, drought, and temperature extremes. To provide genetic material for developing new crop varieties, germ plasma banks of traditional plants will be maintained. Some attention will be given to the development of hydroponics, the cultivation of plants in a medium of fertilized water, rather than in soil.

We must be careful to use a variety of plant types and not become over-dependent on a single variety that might be suddenly devastated by the emergence of a new plant disease or insect pest. The loss of diversity is a serious problem. In the late 19th century, Australian consumers could choose among 450 variety of pears. Today, no more than five are commonly available. The case is similar with other fruits and vegetables. It is especially important to preserve existing wild varieties, mostly found in Third World countries. Even with modern genetic technology, genes to improve crop plants must come from existing wild varieties.

In the United States, between 1945 and 1975 an area of farmland the size of Nebraska was covered with asphalt. Each year fertile farmland, twice the area of Delaware, is converted to highways and other urban use. To quote Gary Gardner, the best soil conservation practices in the world are of little use to cropland that is paved over. This will not be a problem in Uniworld. With its small stable population, primarily urban-based, there will be no suburban sprawl.

Famine and malnutrition will be an historical footnote. Uniworld will comfortably be able to provide adequate food for everyone then and for future generations.

Science

Uniworld does not depend on great scientific break-throughs. We don't need to exceed the speed of light or build a perpetual motion machine. Uniworld can succeed even if we never are able to build a nuclear-fusion electric generator, figure out how to transmit electric power without wires, or conquer cancer.

Uniworld is not anti-science or anti-technology. For an efficient economy, Uniworld needs to use the best that science and technology can offer to attain its goal of a good standard of living for everyone. Uniworld would not have been possible 200 years ago - we didn't have the science and technology then that we need. But we have enough technology now; Uniworld can succeed using only what is already available, but of course we will benefit by continued advances in science and technology.

Uniworld might have been possible 60 years ago or even 90 years ago. We didn't have computers then, but in many respects it would have been easier. The world population was much smaller and the environment, outside of the urban areas, was in much better condition. But here we are at the end of the 20th century and this is where we need to start.

Even though success does not depend on new scientific breakthroughs, Uniworld will strongly encourage scientific research. The developments in science and technology in the past 100-150 years have been astounding, and it is reasonable to expect continued new developments.

However just because we know how to do something, doesn't necessarily mean we should do it. Unfortunately much of the research and development of recent years has been directed toward more efficient killing techniques: nuclear bombs, military missiles, mines, poison gases, bacterial agents, and others. Uniworld research is to help people, not kill people.

We will continue to improve the capability of computers and electronic communication and data transfer. This does not depend on new fundamental scientific breakthroughs; only perfecting what we already know. But the semi-conductor industry is only about 50 years old and it is likely there will be major developments in the next 50-100 years.

Another very important scientific area is Genetics. The Human Genome project in less than 10 years will complete the mapping of the 100,000 genes that affect the growth and function of the human body. We will soon learn the role of many of the genes, how a gene might be replaced by another, how a gene might be inactivated. Eventually we may be able to ensure that every new-born infant is healthy and to combat most diseases.

Related to genetic research are other areas of medical research. To assist in limiting population, we need effective and safe long-term contraceptive methods. Drugs will be a major societal problem until we can find a good way to treat and cure addiction. And of course we will pursue aggressive research on preventing and treating all the major health problems of cancer, stroke, cardiac diseases, AIDS, malaria, diabetes, and others.

Solar energy will be another major study. Today our principal energy source is fossil fuels. We can't manufacture fossil fuels - we are simply mining what nature has created - and before many years the supply will be exhausted. Solar photovoltaic generation of electricity is our most promising energy source to replace fossil fuels.

Writing in Technology Review (July 1997) Robert Hazen and Maxine Singer listed 14 major questions confronting scientists today:

1. What is dark matter?
2. What will be the ultimate fate of the universe?
3. Can we devise a theory of everything?
4. How do atoms combine?
5. Will we run out of energy?
6. What's going on inside the Earth?
7. How many people can the Earth sustain?
8. How did life on Earth originate?
9. Can we unravel the genetic code?
10. How did life on Earth become so varied?
11. How do we develop from a single cell?
12. What are the physical origins of memory?
13. Is behavior dictated by genes?
14. Are we alone in the universe?

Other scientists will offer a different list of questions, though it is likely that many of these questions - such as whether we are alone in the universe and the ultimate fate of the universe - will appear on most lists. Uniworld has its own answer to some of these questions. How many people can the Earth sustain? Uniworld says two billion. Will we run out of energy? We will run out of fossil fuels, but solar energy will replace it, at least until the Sun burns out.

The others are all wonderful questions, many with philosophical and theological implications, but except for the questions about genetics and how atoms combine, they do not affect the successful functioning of Uniworld.

CHAPTER EIGHT
HEALTH CARE, GENETICS, LONGEVITY

Health Care
Universal health insurance

It is not difficult to theorize a health insurance plan; the problem is how to pay for it. If cost were not a limitation, it would be easy to provide a wonderful medical care system for everyone, but in the real world, cost sets limits.

In Uniworld, the government will provide free cradle-to-grave health insurance. Of course, nothing is ever free; someone must pay for it. We pay taxes to enable the government to provide certain services, and universal health insurance is one of these government services.

The government does not provide the medical services, but rather administers the insurance program and makes payments to the health care providers: the doctors, hospitals, pharmacists, nursing homes, and other players in the health care industry.

The doctors and the others are in private practice and are not government employees. If you require medical services you go to the doctor of your choice. The doctor is reimbursed by the government insurance plan in accordance with a standard schedule of payments for each kind of medical service or procedure. It is similar to Medicare payments except that it covers all ages, not just seniors.

Cost of medical services

The doctor is reimbursed by the government according to the standard schedule, but the doctor is permitted to charge the patient more, if he so chooses. Even though the doctor may charge what he pleases, the operation of the free market prevents an exorbitant charge, assuming there is no shortage of doctors.

Every doctor is listed on the Uninet, along with information about his education and medical specialty, and also his fee schedule. If fee is stated as "standard", it means the doctor charges same amount he is reimbursed by the insurance plan; if "standard + 10%" he charges 10% more than standard. He may charge 100% over standard or any amount he wishes, but he will need to be an exceptional doctor to command such a high fee or he will have no patients.

All patients are polled every six months about level of satisfaction with their physician. This information in the form of a composite patient satisfaction score is shown on the physician's listing on the Uninet. Only physicians with the highest satisfaction score will be able to charge much above standard. Most physicians will charge standard or close to it, but this system makes it possible for the superior physician to be rewarded by a higher income.

Cost control

It will be impossible for today's world to provide good universal cradle-to-grave health care for everyone. Uniworld, with its efficient economy and waste reduction, can, but even in Uniworld costs must be controlled. Medical technology is advancing rapidly, and all this improved capability comes with a price tag. Prior to the last 200 years, physicians could do very little. The best physician is one that did little harm and allowed the body to cure itself if it could. Now we have CAT scans, MRI, ultrasound, hip joint replacements, organ replacements, angioplasty, radiation therapy, chemotherapy, and many others still to come.

We will discuss in the following some ways that might be helpful in controlling costs.

Patient co-pay

If medical treatment and hospital care are completely free, some persons will abuse the system by demanding every imaginable test and treatment, even though completely unnecessary. But who decides whether the procedure is necessary or unnecessary? Since the physician is paid by fee-for-service, he has the incentive to call it necessary. The simplest way to resolve this dilemma is to require a patient co-pay. We propose a co-pay of 20% for all medical services.

Some illnesses are unavoidable, at least to the limits of current medical knowledge, but other illnesses can be attributed to poor health habits. If the illness is the fault of the patient, perhaps the co-pay should be 40%, rather than the standard 20% co-pay. But this presents a problem since it is often not clear whether the medical problem is or is not the fault of the patient. For some conditions it is clear the patient is at fault, for example AIDS from unprotected sex. However there is a large gray zone and for many illnesses the patient is only partly at fault, and for many others we just don't know. To avoid complexity, co-pay will be 20% for everyone.

Some serious illnesses require a long series of expensive treatments and medications costing thousands of dollars each month. A co-pay of 20% may be a heavy burden on the financial resources of the patient. After the patient has incurred co-payments of say $5,000 in a calendar year, all subsequent co-pays the balance of the year will be 10% instead of 20%.

But how can a poor person pay $5,000 a year, and possibly more, for medical care? Keep in mind that we are describing here the medical care of Uniworld in which everyone has at least a good minimum income and everyone is covered by universal medical insurance.

It might be necessary to restrict or even not permit private supplemental health insurance that would cover patient co-pay, since this insurance tends to defeat the purpose of co-pay, which is to discourage unnecessary use of medical services.

Expense limit to age 70

In addition to patient co-pay, a related method of controlling costs is to set an expense limit to age 70. Suppose the expense limit is $500,000. A newborn baby starts off with a $500,000 medical expense account. As each medical expense is paid by the government insurance fund, the amount is subtracted from the patient's account. Up until age 70, the patient has the regular insurance coverage even if the $500,000 has been completely expended. However after age 70, the insurance fund will no longer pay for certain high costs medical procedures if the expense limit has been reached. The patient then has the option of paying for it himself or electing a lower cost procedure that is covered by the health plan.

The purpose is to reward those that try to limit medical expense. By avoiding unnecessary expense, it is more likely his account will have an unexpended balance at age 70, and consequently he will continue to have full health insurance coverage after age 70.

Rationing of health care

Rationing of health care is a modern problem. In the 18th century, an ill patient either got well or died. Today we have ill patients that we can't cure but we can keep alive, sometimes for decades, and at great cost.

When the Lakeberg siamese twins were born in 1993 sharing a single heart and liver, experts recognized there was less than a 1% chance that even one twin would survive a tricky separation operation. The surgery was performed but eventually both died, leaving behind 1.3 million in medical bills.

While insurers routinely refuse to pay for new therapy that could save lives, most refuse to "pull the plug" on comatose patients. Some 35,000 US adults and children are living in a persistent vegetative state, some for decades, with bills running into the millions. But families, doctors, and hospital ethic boards hate to consider cost when deciding these cases. Aggressive efforts have been made to keep alive the infant known as "Baby K" who will never hear, see, feel or be conscious, while the costs rapidly mount.

Heroic efforts made to save premature babies weighing less than 1.3 pounds are rarely successful and one third of those that do survive are permanently disabled, even after spending months in neonatal ICUs at costs as high as $2,000 a day.

Our goal is that every baby is born healthy and stays healthy its entire life until time of death. Every pregnant woman will have the embryo tested as early as possible, and if a serious genetic disorder is found, the pregnancy will be terminated. Later it might be possible to check the fertilized ova in vitro for genetic defects before pregnancy is even started.

To terminate life before a baby is born, or better yet before pregnancy even begins, is far preferable than to be confronted with such a life-death decision for a living person. If a patient is comatose, with no possibility of recovery, Uniworld will let that patient die.

Down syndrome is a common genetic defect. If detected early in pregnancy, pregnancy will be terminated, but if detected after birth, Uniworld health insurance will provide health care.

But we have here a very difficult dilemma, that will become increasingly difficult with advances in medical science. Assume a 16 year old boy with an incurable disease that can be held in abeyance by medication costing $100,000 a month. With this medication, the boy can function normally and will live a full life-span. Without this medication, the boy will die within 3 weeks. To keep this boy alive for 64 years, assuming he dies at age 80, will cost the taxpayers more than $76 million. What should be done? Would it matter if he was the only case of its kind or if there were 1,000 similar cases? Suppose the cost was $1 million a month instead of $100,000 a month?

This is a difficult ethical decision that we wish we could avoid. Can we put a price on human life? The answer, unfortunately, is yes, we sometimes must put a price on human life. There is a limit of how much society can be reasonably expected to pay. While we are helping one person, we are jeopardizing the quality of life of hundreds of others.

Medical research

Uniworld will heavily support medical research to develop improved ways to prevent and treat cancer, heart disease, stroke, diabetes, kidney failure, and other diseases. If a disease can be prevented, Uniworld will benefit by a substantial cost saving that would otherwise be required in treating the disease. Medical research however is a two-edged sword in regard to cost savings. Improved but costly treatment may save the life of a patient that previously would have simply died. However improved treatment does not necessarily increase costs; in some instances the new treatment will be quicker and less costly.

By the year 2000, the total cost to the global economy of the AIDS pandemic could reach $514 billion. Sub-Saharan Africa has 70% of the world's cases. the United Nations estimates that by the year 2010, AIDS will reduce Africa's overall labor force by 25%. In Uganda some companies are hiring and training two workers for every job in the hope that one will stay healthy. The lifetime costs of treating someone in the United States with HIV/AIDS is $119,000, and indirect costs of lost productivity and wages are seven times as much.

Children in the Third World die by the millions every year from pneumonia, measles, and other easily addressed diseases for want of a few cents worth of medicine. In Pakistan 15 cents will buy a packet of nutrients that can prevent a child from dying of diarrhea, yet that government spends 31% of its budget on armed forces and weapons, and only 1% goes to health.

Alzheimer's disease has become a major problem for our aging population. By age 85 almost 50% of the elderly have the disease. Recent research indicates the possibility of detecting the disease by genetic testing and PET scanning 20 years before obvious symptoms appear. If so, treatment could start early before the brain has been totally destroyed.

Infectious diseases - bacterial, viral, parasitic - most of which are largely preventable, killed more than 17 million people worldwide in 1995. The leading killers were pneumonia, influenza, diarrhea, tuberculosis, malaria, hepatitis, AIDS, and measles.

Each year 120,000 children are born in the US with birth defects. In addition to the family grief and the diminished quality of life for the victim there is a heavy economic cost: the average lifetime costs for cerebral palsy is estimated as $503,000; for Down's syndrome $451,000.

Scientists thought antibiotics would vanquish infectious diseases but now the bugs are fighting back. The first antibiotic, penicillin, was discovered by Arthur Fleming in 1928. In 1946, just five years after penicillin came into wide use with World War ll, doctors discovered staphylococcus that was invulnerable to the drug. No problem: pharmacologists discovered new antibiotics. These beat down the microbes once again, but soon resistant microbes appeared capable of resisting the new drugs. And so it went, new mutants, new drugs, with the drugs retaining a slight lead. In the 1980s the perception was we had conquered almost every infectious disease, but the victory celebration was premature. Every disease-causing bacterium now has versions that resist at least one antibiotic, and some resist all but one. In 1992, 13,300 hospital patients died of bacterial infections that resisted the antibiotics.

It was not that they had infections immune to every single drug, but rather that by the time doctors found a drug that would work, the attacking bacteria had poisoned the patient's blood or scarred some vital organ.

The financial toll is also steep. Because the first prescribed antibiotic often fails, the patient has to try several. Still more disturbing, it has been found that microbes can share their resistant gene with unrelated microbes, or can become resistant to antibiotics they never encountered.

We must avoid overuse of antibiotics and patients must complete the full scheduled treatment. Some stop after a few days after the most susceptible invaders have been killed, but leaving the more resistant survivors to flourish. We also must limit the use of antibiotics for farm animals.

If we rotate antibiotics, giving some a rest, more vulnerable strains of microbes will re-emerge. This is another important advantage of Uniworld's world government. The government can put certain antibiotics on a do-not-use list for a number of years, then later on reinstate them when they are found once again to be effective. Concurrently the antibiotics that previously were in active use, then go on the do-not-use list, and the rotation cycle continues. A program of this kind is not possible in today's 185 independent-nation world.

Health education

Health education is an important method of reducing medical expense. Health education will be part of the school curriculum from kindergarten through high school. A health counselor on the school staff will confer individually with each student at least once a year to discuss diet, exercise, and other subjects relating to health. A similar no-charge plan will be available for adults.

Programs about health will run frequently on TV and in the newspapers. Extensive health related information will be available on the

Uninet. Neighborhood community centers will feature exercise programs and other health-related activities and encourage participation.

Prevention

Many illnesses might be prevented or treated more easily if detected early. This benefits the individual and also saves medical expense. Uniworld will provide at no charge and without any co-pay certain medical tests such as mammogram for breast cancer, PSA test for prostate cancer, blood glucose test for diabetes, eye pressure test for glaucoma, and others. Every family will have their own blood pressure test device, which is easily used without professional assistance.

Genetics

Uniworld will make extensive use of genetics to reduce health care costs by reducing frequency of inherited diseases. However we must avoid the misuses of the past 'Eugenics" movement and the Nazi "superman" projects.

DNA - the double helix

The discovery of the double-helix structure of DNA by Watson and Crick in 1953 was a major turning point in microbiology. The 23 chromosomes inside every cell of the human body (except red blood cells) contain 3 billion bits of information, called nucleotides, that make up the genetic code. There are only four types of nucleotides (adenine, thymine, guanine, and cytosine) linking together the two parallel strands of the double helix, but they are arranged in many different sequences. Most of the nucleotides are in long, repetitive sequences that seem to serve structural or regulatory purposes, but about 100,000 stretches of the DNA are genes that determine our individual characteristics.

The double helix of DNA resembles a twisted ladder with side pieces made of sugar and phosphates, and closely-spaced connecting rungs. Each rung, called a base pair, consists of a pair of complimentary chemicals, the nucleotides, connected end to end. The nucleotides are mutually attractive: adenine(A) to thymine(T); guanine(G) to cytosine(C). When DNA separates during cell division, coming apart at the middle of each rung like a zipper, an exposed T half-rung on one side of the ladder will always attract an A floating free in the cell, until a double helix, each identical to the original DNA molecule is formed. Each of the four nucleotide bases represent a letter in the genetic code; three letters spell a "word". which are instructions to the cells on how to assemble the amino acids into proteins. A segment of the DNA chain that contains the instructions for a complete protein is called a gene.

Human genome project

When the Human Genome Project was started in 1988 only 400 of those human genes had been identified and located, and less than 1% of the nucleotides had been deciphered. By mid 1995, a research team at the Whitehead Institute for Biomedical Research had created a very rough outline of 90% of the human genome; 35,000 human genes had been identified, 7,500 of which had been located. With new techniques, using gene splicing and gene chopping mechanisms, it is expected the entire project will be completed by the year 2000 or sooner.

Most of the interest is directed at genes thought to cause diseases, about 879 of which have been found or at least hinted at, including several types of cancer, Huntington's disease, cystic fibrosis, schizophrenia, Alzheimer's, and others. Also certain human attributes have allegedly been traced to specific genes including color vision, obesity, homosexuality.

Eventually it is believed each individual's entire personal genome sequence can be stored on a single CD-ROM disk. Within 20 years it is predicted each American will carry a card about the size of a credit card containing his entire genome and medical history. By reading out this card on a computer your physician will have a valuable starting point in dealing with your medical problem.

Heredity theory

Modern genetic science began in the mid-1800s with experiments by Gregor Mendel, an Austrian monk, in cross-breeding a vegetable, the

145

simple pea. Previously the accepted notion of heredity was that the offspring is a blend of the characteristics of each parent. Mendel showed that each parent might contribute one or the other of two possible groups of genetic material and they are combined randomly.

The cell contains 23 pairs of chromosomes. When sperm cells and egg cells are formed they each contain only one member from each chromosome pair. Thus babies inherit 23 chromosomes from each parent. As proven by Mendel, some of the inherited genes are recessive (blue eyes, for example) and some are dominant (brown eyes for example). A baby will show the recessive trait(blue eyes) only if he inherits the recessive gene from both parents. If he inherits the recessive gene from one parent and the dominant gene (brown eyes) from the other parent, the baby will have brown eyes.

But there are exceptions, though rare, to the Mendelian principles of inheritance. Both chromosomes of a pair might come from the same parent, instead of one from each. For some genes it might make a difference whether the gene came from the mother or came from the father. Also the mitochondria within the cell contains its own genetic material, which is subject to mutation, and can affect the genetic material in the cell nucleus.

Mitochondria are considered to be descendants of air-breathing bacteria. Perhaps 5 billion years ago they were engulfed by the progenitors of mammalian and plant cells, becoming a part of these organisms. Over a period of perhaps 500 million years, most of the mitochondria's genetic material emigrated to the nucleus of the cell, leaving behind only 35 genes. Mitochondria have an unique trait in being transferred only in the mother's egg, not in the father's sperm. This characteristic has allowed molecular scientists to trace the genetic ancestry of modern humans to a single woman, an African Eve, who lived in Africa 200,000 years ago.

Genetic engineering

Once a harmful gene has been identified, the next logical step is gene therapy: adding a missing gene or removing a bad gene. Despite a hundred or more experimental attempts prior to 1996 to add a missing gene, none have succeeded, nor is it known how to remove a defective gene. It is believed eventually there will be some success, but it may take years.

Meanwhile an easier alternative approach to genetic engineering is genetic selection of the test tube-fertilized human egg before it is implanted in a woman's uterus. Using pre-implantation diagnosis (PID) geneticists can screen pre-embryos, destroying those pre-embryos that carry undesirable traits or genes. This approach, called germ line therapy, is highly controversial.

Another socially volatile approach to gene therapy is modification of animal tissue for use in human beings. By altering pig DNA it might be possible to engineer swine livers or hearts so they could be transplanted into people without immune system rejection.

We are probably 20 years away from viable modes of gene replacement or alteration, but meanwhile a terrible gap will be created. We have a vast amount of information about our personal genetic makeup, including the probability of contracting some very undesirable disease, but without the ability to do anything about it.

A genetic profile, unless completely confidential, may disclose information that will be a handicap when applying for employment or health insurance, but not in Uniworld. The universal health insurance covers everyone equally, regardless of risk of illness. Everyone has a job and the employer is not concerned about health risk because the employer does not provide company health insurance.

There are a number of techniques used in genetic manipulation. A common method is In Vitro Fertilization: an egg and sperm are combined in a laboratory dish. If the egg is fertilized, the resulting embryo is transferred into the woman's uterus. Another method is "Intracytoplasmic sperm injection". Using a microscopic pipette, a single sperm from a man's ejaculate is injected into an egg and the fertilized egg is similarly transferred into the woman's uterus.

In twinning, a human embryo is allowed to grow until it contains about 8 cells and the embryo is then physically cut into several pieces with a scalpel. When each new embryo has reached a stage containing about 32 cells it can then be transferred to a woman's uterus and carried to term.

Specialists can remove a cell from a fertilized embryo, still in the petri dish, and biopsy it, looking for genetic markers that reveal the presence of some inheritable diseases. An alternate, and probably cheaper method, is to use amniocentesis or chorionic villi sampling. This however poses some risk to the fetus because a biopsy needle must be inserted into the womb. It has been proposed that the genetic test could be made more safely and at less cost by testing the small number of fetal cells that leak into the mother's blood stream during the first trimester, provided an efficient method could be devised to separate the fetal blood cells from the mother's.

Sperm are routinely frozen today for a variety of purposes, including breeding of cattle, preserving endangered species, and artificial insemination of humans. It is also used to preserve the reproductive ability of males prior to cancer therapy. Bull sperm survives well but for men sperm survival is quite variable. It has been reported recently that spermatogonia, the tissues that produce the sperm, can be easily frozen and stored for long periods. Spermatogonia are incredibly productive; a human male produces 1,000 sperm every second from puberty to old age, and every one is different.

Ethical questions: Should a person who has a genetic defect be allowed to undergo a procedure to remove that defect? Should the person be allowed to undergo a procedure to ensure that the defect will not be passed on? Should scientists be allowed to conduct research to alter or improve characteristics of the human species? Should pig livers be implanted into alcoholics? Use of fetal tissue? Cloning of humans? Should embryos be made solely for research purposes? One guideline says embryo research should be limited to a maximum of 14 days, at which point the "primitive streak" appears, indicating the beginning of development of individual organs.

The current practice of In Vitro fertilization is to transfer the embryo to the uterus after about 3 days growth in the laboratory, when it consists of about 6 to 10 cells. A recent report suggests it might be preferable to let the embryo evolve to the blastocyst stage, 50 to 100 cells, before implanting. The chance of survival is better and this also allows more accurate pre-implantation genetic testing for inheritable diseases such as cystic fibrosis, Huntington's disease, Down's syndrome, sickle cell anemia, Tay-Sach's disease, and neural tube defect.

Because of the limited availability of human organs for transplant, many patients die waiting for an available organ, so the use of animal organs is being studied, primarily baboons and pigs. A major problem of course is overcoming rejection response of the body. Moreover baboon organs may contain viruses that are harmless in their normal host, but may be deadly when transplanted into a human. The AIDS epidemic almost certainly started when an African villager ate a monkey that carried the virus. Baboons are also expensive, they take a long time to raise to adulthood, and their organs are often too small for adult humans. Pigs are probably better candidates. The risk of viral disease is low since humans have been eating pigs for thousands of years. Pigs are inexpensive, have large litters, are easy to raise, and mature quickly. Their organs are the right size, and researchers believe they have found a way to overcome rejection of organs from pigs.

The Jukes and the Kallikaks were the degenerate families of the early eugenics movement. The popular idea is that good and bad character traits and destinies are the consequences of good and bad genes. The most complicated human behavior is blamed on DNA or "tainted blood": success or failure, kindness or cruelty, criminality, anti-social behavior, alcoholism, aggression, timidity, arson, and almost every aspect of human behavior and personality, even church attendance.

It is true of animals that certain behavior is genetically determined such as survival instincts and mating rituals. Border collies herd sheep in a unique characteristic way whether they have been trained or not, even if they have never seen sheep before. Aggressive and nurturing behavior of mice can be manipulated with adjustments of hormone levels, but this does not support the popular idea that genes determine such complex human personality traits as success, failure, political preference, or criminality.

A 1965 study found that a disproportionate number of men in an Edinburgh correctional institution were XYY males instead of the normal XY. It was suggested the extra Y chromosome predisposes its carrier to aggressive behavior, but this conclusion is not generally accepted.

Common observation shows that alcoholism runs in families, but many traits run in families, poverty or bad manners for example, without being a consequence of heredity. The prevalence of alcoholism in some families could reflect role models, the availability of alcohol, or the reaction to abuse. It is easy to understand the appeal of bad genes as the explanation for anti-social behavior. This is something that can perhaps be corrected by genetic engineering rather than the uncertain route of social reform. The idea of genetic predisposition encourages a passive attitude toward social injustice, an apathy about continuing social problems, and a reason to preserve the status quota. Genetics contends that individuals succeed or fail, not because of their efforts or social circumstances, but because they are genetically programmed for their fate. And if behavior is completely pre-determined, either by genetics or by environment, then the criminal cannot really be blamed.

We are the product of nature and nurture, heredity and environment. The science of genetics in the coming centuries will enable us to direct and regulate our nature and our heredity. It will be a powerful tool for creating a better world, but we must be careful to use it wisely.

Life-Span Limit
In this section we will discuss what will probably be the most controversial proposal in Uniworld: the need to limit life-span.

Life-span is increasing
Biologists once believed that properly nurtured cells could live forever in a laboratory, but it is now recognized that cells age and die, after about 50 cell divisions.

Research is under way to increase life span of certain animals and possibly apply the findings to prolonging human life. Canadian researchers have recently discovered a set of genes that determines the life span of the common nematode, a microscopic transparent worm composed of exactly 959 cells. By crossbreeding worms with certain mutations of these genes, one of the mutants lived two months, as opposed to the normal 9 days. This mutant looked and behaved normally but it ate less and moved more slowly. The prevalent theory of aging is that it is caused by the accumulated damage to the DNA from the highly-reactive byproducts of metabolism.

Some medical researchers view death as a medical accident, correctable with enough money, will, and scientific ingenuity. We should emphasize preventative medicine, rather than rescue medicine and accept the need to ration health care, not just to control costs, but to curb our insatiable appetite for longer lives. Death should be viewed, not as an accident that medicine has failed to eliminate, but as a natural part of the human condition. In 1965 Social security and Medicare took 14% of the federal budget; now 34% and rising. The US Census Bureau counted 35,808 people 100 years and older in 1990, double the number of 10 years before, and there could be 1,000,000 by 2080. Improved health habits will extend life but there is no evidence that diet and exercise can ameliorate the ravages of Alzheimer's disease, Parkinson's disease, and other illnesses that primarily strike the elderly. Now about 1% of the US population is older than 85, but by the year 2050 up to 20% of the population may be that old. Americans over 65 make up only about 13% of the nation's population today, yet they account for more than one third of all health spending, fill 40% of all hospital beds, and consume twice as much prescription medication as all other age groups combined. We may have 150-year-old people, but they may spend the last 40 years in a nursing home.

For centuries, Asia's population charts have looked like a pyramid with a wide base of people under 15 supporting a narrower band of the middle aged, topped by a tiny sliver of the elderly. But the percentage of people over 60 has been steadily increasing due to increased longevity and reduced birth rate. In Singapore, each retired person is now supported by 8 workers; by 2030 there will be only 2 workers per retiree.

The age span now is primarily between infancy and about 80 years. As medical sciences continues to extend the life span, it will soon extend into the 90's, then 100, 110, and 120, with no known limit in sight. About half of the world population will be older than 60 years.

More than 25% of all Medicare expense is incurred during the last year of life. If medical technology is able to keep patching us up so we can keep breathing an extra 40 years, the medical cost may become so huge as to seriously degrade the standard of living for everyone. And where will it stop? There may not be any limit to how long life can be extended. The instinct of self-preservation, the desire to cling to life, is built into our basic nature. If the life span is extended to 120 years, why not 140 years? Maybe we can reach 200 years! Until there is a change in our inherent nature, no matter how many years we have lived, we still want to go on longer. The end result may be a complete collapse of the health insurance system.

These old people of age 110 and older are still alive and breathing but they will not be healthy and vigorous. They will be living corpses with half of their vital organs and structural elements - heart, liver, kidneys, hip joints, and others - animal transplants or synthetic substitutes.

Life-span 80 year average

Objective is to keep people in good health and feeling well until it is time to die, but Uniworld's advanced medical technology will make possible a greatly extended life span, possibly to age 140 or longer.

The population of Uniworld will be stabilized at two billion persons. The advances in medical knowledge is steadily increasing the average life span. Originally the lengthened average life span was primarily due to the decrease in infant mortality, but now more and more people are living into the 80's, 90's, and older. If the death rate is decreasing, we must reduce the birth rate proportionately to maintain a two billion population.

In Uniworld the average life span will be 80 years, and it will not be increased beyond 80 years. Note the reference to an average life span. It does not mean that everyone drops dead on his 80th birthday. Some will die before 80, some will live into their 90's and older, same as now. Unless we can modify human nature, it would be an emotional nightmare if everyone lived to exactly age 80. We look at the calendar and keep marking off our remaining days. In our present society, we realize we are not immortal, but no matter how old we are, we always think that perhaps we can last another year or two.

Life span for men and women will be 80 years average -some may die at age 70, a few may live to 95 and older, but the average will be 80. The few that die before age 70 will primarily be accidental deaths.

How to limit life-span

In many primitive societies it is the custom of the tribe that an elderly person, at a certain age, will leave the tribe and go off to die. This is not cruelty but an accepted custom of the tribal society. The tribe's marginal existence, its struggle to survive, makes it impossible to support and care for the non-productive old. Uniworld is not a primitive society and will provide for millions of the non-productive old, but even Uniworld has limitations.

Here are several possible ways to limit life-span to an average of 80 years:

  a. restriction on medical treatment
  b. genetic engineering so that 80 years is natural life-span
  c. trigger death at age 80 average

Restriction on medical treatment

In this scenario, we would deliberately prohibit all organ transplants and all medical technology developed after the year 2000, except for relief of pain. Without new medical advances, life expectancy would stabilize at the present level of about 80 years. This is not acceptable.

Genetic engineering to limit life-span

In this scenario, we will be genetically conditioned to live to an average of 80 years, regardless of advances in medical technology. This would be a good solution, but very difficult to achieve. More likely, advances in medical technology would continue to increase the life span, requiring further adjustments in the genetics to counter it. Sounds good in theory but may not be possible.

Death triggered at average of 80 years

At first hearing, this proposal is outrageous and horrible, nothing less than murder.

This is how it might work: At birth a microchip with your personal identification number and date of birth is imbedded in your brain. Each day a Master Computer with a random number generator selects a birth-date, no more recent than 70 years earlier. All those born on that date will die within the following 30 days.

This date is entered into a Date Control Computer along with the identification number of every one born on that date. If this is your date of birth, you have a maximum of 30 days till you must die. This gives you time to get your financial affairs in order, update your will, and bid farewell to family and friends. You then enter into the Date Control Computer when you wish to die. The Date Control Computer will cause your death painlessly that night when you are asleep by actuating the microchip in your brain. If you do not notify the Date Control Computer you will die on the 30th day.

The computer program is designed to adjust for increased proba-bility of death as we get older, and also provide an average life span of 80 years. A 95 year old is more likely to die within the next 12 months than a 75 year old, yet it is still possible the 95 year old will outlive the 75 year old.

This proposal, date of death controlled by a computer, sounds like some monstrous thing out of George Orwell's "1984", but if viewed objectively, it mirrors our present world. No one lives forever, we all die sooner or later. Our risk of dying increases as we grow older, some will die at 71, more will die at 75, a few will not die till 101 or even older.

We know we will die eventually, but, except for suicide, we do not know when. It will be the same in Uniworld; we will not know when we will die - not until the date is selected by the Master Computer. If at age 20 we could find out the exact date of our eventual death, most of us would prefer not to know.

This will be better than our present world, because we will be able to utilize all the advances in medical technology to keep us healthy and vigorous our entire life, and yet maintain an 80 year average life-span. However, as discussed in the previous section, we may need to put some restrictions on super-expensive medical procedures after age 70. The emphasis will be to add to the quality of life, not the length of life.

Comment on life-span limit

Man, like all other animals, is born with the instinct of self-preservation. We resist death. However when we are terminally ill and in great pain, we may accept death as a welcome friend, a release from suffering. In Uniworld, with the advantage of improved medical technology, most of us will be well and vigorous until the day the Master Computer selects our birth-date and says we must now die. This is a psychological difficulty. Perhaps genetic engineering will be able to diminish somewhat our instinct of self-preservation after age 70.

The urge to keep living may be so strong that many may object to limiting life span to an average of 80 years when it is scientifically possible to substantially lengthen the life span. Rather than extending life span by creating old people half human and half synthetic replacement parts, perhaps it might be better to create a twin.

We start by in vitro fertilization in a petri dish. The fertilized egg is split into identical twins. one of the twins, which is you, is transplanted into your mother's womb. Nine months later you are born in the usual way and you live to about age 80. Instead of extending your life span, you die. Meanwhile however your twin, the other fertilized egg, had been held dormant in a frozen state. At your death, your twin is activated and it lives another 80 years. In effect you and your identical twin have lived a total of 160 years. Of course this is not quite the same as your living 160 years since your twin, even though it has the same genes, is another individual and not you, and there is no memory continuity. But it does avoid all those old half-synthetic people.

The reason it is necessary to limit life span is the economic and social burden of a constantly increasing number of very old people. But suppose medical science found a way to slow down aging, a fountain of youth. At age 120 we would be just as active mentally and physically as we are now at age 60, and a life span of 160 years became feasible. Would this be good?

Somehow a world with so many very old people is not ideal; it distorts the balance and the rhythm of the life cycle. Consider an 80 year life cycle: the first 25 years is growth from infancy into adulthood and education; the next 25 years is marriage and children; the next 15 years is the empty-nest stage and career wrap-up, and final 15 years is retirement, ending in death at about 80. But if life span is increased to average of 160 years, the final stage, retirement, will become 95 years, instead of 15.

Of course as life span increases it is likely that normal retirement will be postponed to a later age. But this still distorts the life cycle. We will have 25 years for growing to adulthood and education, 25 years for raising a family, and then 110 years still to go. If medical science can slow down aging, perhaps it will also slow down growth from infancy to adulthood. Then we will have 50 years for growing to adulthood and education, 50 years for raising a family, 30 years pre-retirement, and 30 years retirement. Is this progress?

But even if we were able to live to ago 160, healthy and vigorous, this does not solve the dilemma, but merely postpones it to an older age. What happens after age 160? We are assuming that advances in medical science has made it possible to keep us in good active health until age 160, not forever. After age 160 our body starts to deteriorate and eventually we die. Will the dying stage be stretched out over the next 10-20 years with replacement of heart, of lungs, of kidneys, of liver, of hip joints, knee joints, and others, until not much of our original parts are left, but at an unsustainable health care cost. This leaves us with the similar alternatives of restricting medical care or triggering death so that the average life span is 160 years. The issue is the same whether life span is limited to an 80 year average or to a 160 year average.

Limit on Physical Size

We are getting bigger

In a previous section we discussed the necessity of limiting life-span; Uniworld might also consider limiting average physical size. Though much less critical an issue than limiting life-span, this has possible advantages, as pointed out by an article in The Futurist, January 1995, by Thomas Samaras.

Pre-historic man was substantially shorter than today's humans. In 1700, the average American man was 5'6"; the average today is 5'10". In Japan, today's adults are 3"-5" taller than their grandparents. If present trends continue, the average adult male will be 6' tall, perhaps by year 2050.

A change from 5' tall to 6' tall is an increase of 20% Along with increase in height will be an increase in weight, but the increase in weight will be considerably greater than 20%. A 5' man might weigh 114 pounds on average, while a 6' man might weigh 171 pounds, an increase of 50% in weight.

Advantage of smaller size

What might be gained if the average adult male was 5-feet tall rather than 6-feet tall? A population of 6-footers, compared to a population of 5-footers, will require more food, larger size clothing, larger furniture, larger homes, larger cars, and larger doses of medication. The larger physical size will put the same pressure on our resources and environment as a population increase of 25-35%.

How to limit human size

We can reduce average human size by reducing food intake. If children do not receive adequate nutrition, they will be smaller as adults. This of course is not acceptable; besides, it would also be counter-productive because poor nutrition will affect health and increase medical costs.

We need to limit human size without degrading health. The most likely way we can do this is by genetic engineering. The science of genetics is still in its infancy, but eventually we might know how to influence human size, probably within the next 50 years.

Optimum human size

We are suggesting here that Uniworld eventually might have a goal of 5'0" average adult male size, and women slightly less. There is no urgency to this; it can be phased in over a period of 200 years or so, once the genetic technology is available, but the savings are worthwhile.

But why stop at 5'0"? If there is a substantial saving in reducing human size to 5'0" average, wouldn't the savings be even greater if average size were reduced to 4"0"? What about 3'0"? How small can we go? What is the optimum size?

We can't answer this question yet. One limitation on size reduction is the affect on the brain. If the skull is too small, this may reduce the space available for the brain, and hence the capability of the brain. We may end up looking like ER or the little green men from Mars, a large head on a tiny body. A goal of 5'0" average size appears reasonable, and will not affect intelligence. Whether Uniworld decides to go smaller will be left to future generations to determine.

CHAPTER NINE
LANGUAGE, RACE, AND RELIGION

Language of Uniworld

Uniworld will have a common world-wide language, spoken and written.

Advantages of a common language

One universal language will facilitate communication among all the peoples of Uniworld and will enable a smoother functioning society. If you and I speak different languages, there is a barrier between us. Worldwide about 2700 different languages are spoken, though of course many are limited to a small geographic area. The public school district of Los Angeles must cope with 150 different languages. In Canada the French-speaking province of Quebec threatens to secede from English-speaking Canada, primarily because of the language issue.

One universal language has economic and social advantages. Newspapers, books, reports, forms need not be duplicated in multiple languages; motion pictures need not have sub-titles; conferences and meetings of diverse groups need not have interpreters. These attempts to cope with language diversity are not only costly but are only partially successful. To limit the cost, the translations can cover only a few major languages, while ignoring dozens of other languages.

Hundreds of languages are spoken in China, and Chinese from one province may be unable to understand those from another province, though fortunately the written language is the same. The government is trying to have Mandarin adopted as the spoken language throughout the country.

The earliest written languages were pictorial in nature - the drawings of the cavemen, the hieroglyphics of the early Egyptians, the ideographs of the Chinese - but modern languages use a phonetic alphabet. The alphabet is an extraordinary invention, the elegant simplicity of its ability to express a wide range of vocal sounds with just 26 -30 characters. Compare this to the 49,000 or so characters, each expressing a different word, that must be learned by a literate reader of Chinese.

The origin of the alphabet is unknown, but apparently was first used by the Phoenicians. The phonemic principle states that any language in the world can be broken down into a limited number of distinctive sounds, usually ranging from 25 to 35. It has been suggested that the signs of the alphabet were originally created to designate the days of the lunar month. By choosing a different sounding word (an animal, object, etc) for each day of the month (30 days) they accidentally invented a phonetic system at the same time. It was later realized that words could be formed by combining the initial sounds of the calendrical words. The 29 or 30 letters of the original Phoenician alphabet dates from the 14th century BC and matches the number of days in the lunar month. The symbols themselves were originally the characters in the ancient lunar zodiac, and eventually simplified to the modern alphabet.

Choice of a common language

Uniworld will have a single common language; which particular language it will be, is less critical. Mandarin Chinese is spoken by more people than any other language, but its ideographic written language is difficult to learn and is not suitable for computer use. The emergence of a language that would unite the world is a dream going back to the late 17th century. In 1887 Dr. Zamenhof created Esperanto, the most popular of the synthetic languages and currently used by 7-12 million people, but neither this or Interlingua or any other man-made language has real roots in any community. Spanish or French would be better, but English is the logical choice.

According to "The Story of English" by McCrum, Cran, and MacNeil, English did not exist when Julius Caesar landed in Britain about 2,000 years ago. Five hundred years later English was a minor language spoken by a handful, and incomprehensible to modern ears. Nearly a thousand years later, at the end of the 16th century, when William Shakespeare was in his prime, English was the native speech of perhaps 5-7 million Englishmen.

But from 1600 to the present, the speakers of English - including

Scots, Irish, Americans, and many others - traveled into every corner of the globe, carrying their language with them. English has a few rivals, but no equals. Neither Spanish, or Arabic, or Russian, or French has its global sway. In many countries where English is not the native language such as Nigeria, Singapore, Indonesia, Philippines, it has become a second language, unifying huge territories and diverse populations. India, with 200 languages, needs English to unify the country.

Of all the world's languages, English has the richest vocabulary. The Oxford English Dictionary lists about 500,000 words, and another 500,000 scientific and technical terms are uncataloged. German has a vocabulary of about 185,000 words, and French fewer than 100,000. Three quarters of the world's mail, cables, and faxes are in English, and more than half of the world's technical and scientific journals. Half of business negotiations in Europe are conducted in English.

English does have some drawbacks - varied pronunciation of its vowels, and its irregular spelling. There are 13 spellings for the "sh" sound. Some efforts have been made to simplify English spelling, but with only limited success.

But English does have some important characteristics. First, unlike French or German, the gender of every noun in English is determined by its meaning and does not require a masculine, feminine or neuter article (der, die, das). Second, English has a grammar of great simplicity and flexibility. Nouns and verbs have simplified word endings. Nouns can become verbs, and verbs nouns, impossible in other languages, as in we can "bus" children to school.

But foremost, the great quality of English is its teeming vocabulary, 80% of which is foreign derived. Because its roots are so varied - Celtic, Germanic, Scandinavian, Dutch, Latin,, French, Spanish, - it has words in common with every language in Europe: German, Yiddish, Dutch, Flemish, Danish, Swedish, French, Italian, Portuguese, Spanish, and Russian. English has borrowed from Hebrew, Arabic, Hindi-Urdu, Bengali, Malay, Chinese, and the languages of Java, Australia, Tahiti, Polynesia. The Indianization and Africanization of English - from the Krio of West Africa, the Singlish of Singapore, and the Pidgin of

Melanesia - is introducing a multi-cultural and innovative element into the language. It is the enormous range and varied sources of this vocabulary, as much as the sheer numbers and spread of its speakers, that makes English a language of such unique vitality.

Because so much of English is foreign derived, there will be less resistance to the choice of English as the universal language than to any other. But there will be strong opposition to the concept of a universal language, regardless of what language is selected. As an interim measure, English might be adopted as a universal secondary language that would co-exist with the language of the region, French, Swahili, or whatever. All schools around the world will teach English as a primary or secondary language and the use of English in daily life will be encouraged. Gradually English will replace the regional language. The full benefits of a universal language will not be realized so long as the regional languages remain in use, but it will be a good starting point.

The acceptance of English to replace all regional languages will be much easier once a world government is in place. Local boundaries will disappear and with it local insularities. The world government can take active steps to facilitate English replacing all other languages, though there will be a brief transition period. Even though English has a huge vocabulary of over 500,000 words, a working knowledge of English is possible with only a few thousand words. No language is static, least of all English. The English of Chaucer is a foreign language to us today. Spelling will be simplified, and some irregular verbs will be modified.

Many of the changes needed to get from where we are now to Uniworld will be difficult and some will take 100-200 years. The adoption of a universal world language is one of the easiest and fastest. Once a world government is in effect, English will be in general world wide use within 25 years.

Race and Ethnicity

In Uniworld all racial and ethnic differences will disappear. All the diverse peoples of the world will be blended into a universal humanity.

Origin of man

Our earliest hominid, about 5.6 million years ago, originated in Africa. Genetic evidence suggests that chimps, gorillas, and humans all descended from a single unknown species that lived 5 million to 7 million years ago. Homo erectus dates from about 1.7 million years ago, Neanderthal Man about 0.5 million years ago, Modern man, Homo sapiens, about 200,000 years ago.

Every man on earth today is related, linked by a Y chromosome to a single common ancestor who lived about 190,000 years ago. A recent study compared the chromosomes of 38 men chosen from different continents and found virtually no differences. Other researchers argue that our ancestors migrated out of Africa more than a million years ago and modern man evolved simultaneously in different parts of the world. However studies of the mitochondria of the cell which is inherited through the maternal side support the theory that all modern humans are descended from a single "African Eve" that lived a few hundred thousand years ago. Most of the evidence indicates that modern man originated in Africa relatively recently, spread into other parts of the world and edged the earlier pre-human groups into extinction.

Races and ethnic groups

"Race" is a vague term difficult to define. In the popular sense it refers to a group of people with a similar physical trait such as skin color, hair type, shape of nose, slant of eyelids, body build, stature, skull shape. Some early anthropologists divided the peoples of the world into three races, others concluded there were more than 30 races. It was later realized that physical differences are superficial, are affected by the environment, and blend into one another. Geneticists define race by noting differences in gene frequencies. The number of distinct races that can be categorized by this method depends upon the particular genetic trait studied.

When a group of people is physically isolated by geographical barriers such as deserts, oceans, mountains, and are also isolated by political and cultural barriers, involuntarily or by choice, they will closely inbreed and share a distinctive gene pool. However such genetic isolation is typically short-lived. In any event only 6% of genetic variation is accounted for by differences between major racial groups. The vast majority of genetic differences among human beings is found in differences from one village to another or one family to another.

Sociologists define race not on basis of biologic or genetic differences but rather as a sociological concept. From this point of view, a race is a group of people who see themselves, and are seen by others, as different because of some physical characteristic, such as skin color.

To most laymen, human beings are divided into a few broad groups based on skin color: white race (Caucasian), black race (Negroid), yellow race (Mongoloid), etc. However each of these groups is further divided into hundreds of ethnic groups. Both categories of race and ethnicity are essentially social definitions, not biological differences. In central Africa people are assigned to the Tutsi or Hutu race on the basis of height. The two have similar skin color and similar features, but the Tutsi are tall, the Hutu short.

The term "race" may be defined as a breeding population whose members share a number of distinctive genetic characteristics. This requires a group that is genetically isolated by social barriers or geographical barriers. In the popular use of the term race, reference is usually made to certain geographical groups such as: Australoids of Australia and New Guinea: large brow ridge, broad nose, skin light chocolate to dark brown, plentiful hair. Caucasoids of Europe and Western Asia: fair-skinned, light-eyed, light-haired, straight or wavy, sharp features, in the North: dark hair, dark eyes, in the South. Mongoloids of Southeast Asia: short stature, broad-faced, black hair, straight and coarse, eyes marked by the epicanthic fold. Negroids of sub-Saharan Africa: skin dark brown or black, dark eyes, spiral head hair, low-bridged nose with flaring nostrils.

The distinguishing physical characteristics listed above are superficial and have little scientific validity. In today's world every so-called race is really a mixture of many ancestral groups. However these external physical differences do classify people and segregate them into separate groups.

Whereas racial categories are based on physical differences, ethnic categories are based on cultural differences. An ethnic group is a category of people who see themselves, and are seen by others, as different because of their cultural heritage. Members of an ethnic group share a common ancestry (real or imagined); language; customs of dress, art, ornamentation, music; family patterns, moral codes, value system; patterns of recreation; religion; loyalty to a cultural tradition. It may or may not have its own political unit.

Advantage of racial and ethnic blending

A key objective of Uniworld is the elimination of war. War is armed conflict between nations, tribes, or groups, while civil war is a war between citizens of one nation. Uniworld is a world government and the prior sovereign nations will become regional administrative governments without armies, similar to the states of our own country. Without nations, war between nations is eliminated.

However civil war is still a possibility, especially if there are distinct identifiable groups in separate geographic areas. These groups might be identified by differences in language, in skin color or other physical characteristic such as hair or eye slant, in religion, in cultural values, in ethnicity, in economic interests. In Northern Ireland the conflict is religious between the Catholics and Protestants. In Rwanda the ethnic conflict between the Tutsi and Hutu tribes has so far slaughtered 500,000 people. The conflict in Yugoslavia among the Serbs, Croats, and Bosnian Muslims is partly religious but is primarily an ethnic civil war. Before the fighting, Bosnian Serbs and Bosnian Muslims lived peacefully side by side, but as the fighting spread people fled and the country split into a separate Serb region and a separate Bosnian Muslim region. The US Civil War is more aptly called a War Between the States because the opposing groups were not commingled but lived in different geographic areas, the North and the South. The causes were cultural differences regarding slavery and economic differences between an industrial North and a plantation-based South.

In Uniworld's one-world government, war between nations is eliminated, but there is still the risk of civil war. If Uniworld is able to provide an efficient economic system with a good standard of living for everyone, without have-nots, there will be little risk of civil war. A single universal world-wide language, as discussed in the previous section, will facilitate communication between people and reduce risk of inter-group conflict.

When racial and ethnic groups live in the same geographic/political unit some of the possible outcomes are: subjugation, segregation, expulsion, or annihilation - all undesirable. A better possible outcome is pluralism or assimilation. Pluralism is the co-existence of separate ethnic and racial groups within a society. It is a philosophy that assumes that minorities not only have rights, but also considers the lifestyle of the minority group to be a desirable way of participating in society. Pluralism is a reaction against assimilation and the melting-pot idea. Pluralism in Switzerland has so far worked very well with its Italian-speaking area, French-speaking area, and German-speaking area, but all strongly pro-Swiss.

Assimilation is the fusion of cultural heritages, the merging of cultures, often involving the rejection of certain ideologies, customs, and language. The process of assimilation seldom operates on a 50-50 basis. One of the societies may have greater prestige, or is more suited to the environment, or has greater numerical strength.

To some, pluralism, the multi-cultural society, is the ideal solution, with individual self-determination and preservation of cultural identity. In Uniworld, our objective is a single universal world-wide culture, not pluralism. In earlier times, diverse cultures could exist successfully in different parts of the world, completely unaware of each other. In more recent times, diverse cultures have co-existed successfully in the same country, particularly in some of the countries of western Europe. But in the long term, multi-cultural societies bear the seeds of potential conflict. Sooner or later - maybe in

30 years, maybe in 130 years - issues will develop that will split the country along ethnic lines. Human nature is not always just, generous, and caring; it can also be selfish and cruel. We can not change human nature, but we can reduce the tendency of the baser side of human nature to assert itself by creating a single unified world-wide society.

The most effective way to eliminate conflicts due to racial and ethnic differences is to eliminate racial and ethnic differences. In Uniworld everyone will be of the same race, the human race, and the same ethnicity. This is the melting pot concept of the pre-First-World-War era. The flood of immigrants from Poland, Russia, Hungary, and other east European countries into the United States were to be merged into the American pool. The assimilation took longer than was expected, but now after several generations these immigrants have been fairly well blended into the general population of the United States. Unfortunately the black population of the US and the more recent Latino and Asian immigrants mostly remain as distinct groups living in segregated neighborhoods and communities.

A controversial issue today in the US is so-called "affirmative action", a program to improve the economic opportunities of minorities. The focus is however primarily on the black population, which admittedly are, on average, at the lower end of the economic scale. Once we have racial blending, this issue will become merely a historical footnote.

Disadvantages of racial and ethnic blending

There is no serious disadvantage to racial and ethnic blending. Some may say we lose our personal identity, our ancestral roots. Not so; our roots are broadened, tied not to just one group, but to many.

Some may say we lose the cultural riches of life style, customs, music, art, and dress developed over hundreds of years. Everything is blended into one mush. Not so; we can preserve whatever is worthwhile saving. The ethnic group will disappear, but we can still enjoy the music, the art, the literature, the unique food, and other interesting lifestyles the group created.

Permanent records of the various cultures will be preserved on film, video tape, photographs, sound recordings, and computer data bases for study by future anthropologists and sociologists. These cultural elements are not destroyed but instead are shared with the entire world. You need not be Spanish to enjoy the art of Picasso, Italian to enjoy the operas of Verdi, German to enjoy the music of Beethoven, English to enjoy the plays of Shakespeare.

However some cultural elements of the many ethnic groups, though noted in the historical record, will have no place in Uniworld. Gladiator fights to the death, human sacrifice, witch burning, feet binding of little girls, etc. were once part of the culture in past eras. In the present day, slavery, women as chattels, and female circumcision are still found in some cultures. Uniworld will keep the best and discard the rest.

It is true that travel to distant lands will be less exciting. The people we see will be the same we see at home - same appearance, same language, similar life style. There will be some variety if only because of difference in climate and geography that affect life style. But we won't see, and we won't miss, the grinding poverty found today in much of sub-Saharan Africa and South Asia and in the shanty towns and slums of many of the large cities around the world.

Yet travel will still give us the opportunities to experience the beauty of nature - snow-capped mountains, roaring waterfalls, giant trees, and wildlife of astonishing variety. And because of the reduced population and the environmental protection of Uniworld, the natural world will be preserved for the continuing enjoyment of the present and future generations.

How to achieve racial and ethnic blending

Race relates to difference in physical appearance; ethnicity relates to difference in culture. We have 5-30 races, depending upon which expert is counting; but hundreds of ethnic groups, so obviously many ethnic groups share the same race.

The only way to merge race is by old-fashioned biology - by inter-racial marriage. However inter-marriage is not necessary to merge ethnic groups of the same race. If it were feasible to remove from their parents all children at 2 years of age and raise them separately as one group, ethnic differences could disappear in one generation, but for many reasons such a program is obviously both impractical and undesirable.

Ethnic groups will merge by inter-marriage, same as racial groups, but the main impetus to blending will be the influence of Uniworld's egalitarian society. Diverse ethnic groups will live in the same neighborhood, go to the same schools, work together, share the same recreational facilities, speak the same language, dress the same, watch the same TV shows. Discrimination against any group will be illegal and determined efforts will be made to avoid segregated neighborhoods. The influence of the universal Uniworld culture will eventually replace the old multi-ethnic cultures.

With a more open society, international trade, international travel, less segregation, open housing, and fewer barriers to immigration, many countries of the world have multi-racial populations. Where people are able to associate freely, the number of mixed marriages will increase. Millions of people around the world are the children of mixed-race marriages, and this trend will continue.

Ethnic differences will disappear eventually even if we do nothing specific to encourage it, but the blending of race requires inter-racial marriage. To accelerate the process, Uniworld will have incentives to encourage mixed-race marriages such as cash awards, education preferences, special privileges, and job preferences.

We would like to blend all these external differences in appearance - shape of nose, type of hair, hair color, eye color, skin color, stature, etc - but it is more feasible to concentrate on just one: skin color. Fortunately many of the other physical differences such as shape of nose and type of hair are associated with skin color difference, so if skin color is blended, certain other features are blended at the same time.

One possibility is to measure the skin color of every teen-ager and assign a number from #1 to #7, from very light to very dark. When that person marries, he and she will both receive a cash bonus or some other incentive depending upon the degree of difference. The greatest bonus of course will be for a 1/7 marriage. Someone with a #4 skin color can't qualify for a 1/7 bonus, but a 4/1 or 4/7 marriage will still earn a bonus.

The first generation inter-racial marriage will meet the most resistance, but after that it will be easy. Assuming everyone qualifies for the maximum bonus, after only one inter-racial generation there will be no more #1, #2, #6, or #7 skin color. Everyone will be #3, #4, or #5.

To facilitate inter-racial marriage, every city in the world must have a population made up of a variety of so-defined racial groups. A marriage of a St. Louis man to a Cairo woman has a major logistic impediment; it is much more likely if they lived in the same city. If we defined four races worldwide, designated as A,B,C, and D, and if the world population is 30% A, 10% B, 20% C, and 40% D, it would be ideal for race blending if every city in the world had each of these four races, and in this ratio.

This of course is not the case. The best we can hope for initially is that every city will at least have a significant representation of each of the four races. Uniworld will encourage people of a racial group in surplus to move to another city that has a shortage.

Religion in Uniworld

A religion is a system of beliefs and practices shared by a group of people that provides a pattern of behavior based on the supernatural and sacred. Religion deals with the ultimate meaning of life. Why are we here? How can we avoid misfortune and evil? What happens after death? Religion is an attempt to cope with the unknown and the unknowable and the uncertainty of life. We want to believe the universe has a purpose, and if so if must have a master planner. Since this is not subject to rigid scientific inquiry, the universe must be the creation of a supernatural power. A philosophy that deals with the same questions of the meaning of life, but without the concept of a supernatural power, is not a religion in the strict sense.

Some form of religion is found in all societies, though specific beliefs and practices vary. Some believe in ghosts of ancestors, in evil spirits; some believe in a single deity, others in many gods. The earliest evidence of religion dates back to Neanderthal man over 60,000 years ago. The Neanderthals buried their dead with great care and provided them with gifts and food for the next world. They also built small altars out of bear bones indicating they conducted rituals seeking supernatural aid.

Religion has varied functions. It brings people together physically, aiding social cohesion; it formalizes tribe group beliefs and values into a set of doctrines; it provides consolation and emotional support at critical stages of the life cycle.

Freedom of Religion

A basic tenet of Uniworld is to minimize the risk of inter-group conflict by minimizing group differences. In Uniworld everyone will speak the same language, have an adequate standard of living, and the same culture. Physical differences in appearance will disappear with inter-racial marriages, racial and ethnic blending. But in one important respect, religious practice, group differences will continue. However Uniworld will have freedom of religion and full tolerance for all religions.

Restrictions on religion

Even though Uniworld will have freedom of religion, there will be some limits on religious expression. Church and state will be kept separate. If a major difference arises between a religious group and secular society, the latter will prevail. Some religious practices, such as polygamy and physical torment, for example, will be banned even if sanctioned by a religion.

Religion might protect the status quo against needed change and may sanctify authoritarianism. A religion may convince itself that it is the only "true" religion, and that all other religions are profane and must be eradicated, as the many religious wars of the past can testify. The Spanish Inquisition of the 13th, 14th, and 15th century is a blot on the history of religion.

Karl Marx called religion the "opiate of the masses". He saw religion as a tool of the upper classes to dominate the lower classes. The lower classes were distracted from taking steps for social change by organized religion's promise of a reward in heaven. Accept the hardships of life - it is only a prelude to eternal bliss. Uniworld is not opposed to belief in an afterlife, but the belief in a hereafter must supplement, not replace, the conviction that our life here and now is also important and our goal is to make it the best possible.

Religion should not be active politically except in regard to an issue that directly affects religion. One religion should not attack another religion verbally, or in print, or in any other form of communication. Proselytizing through the media is acceptable, but not coercive direct proselytizing or brainwashing. Religious activity shall be confined to religion and not branch out into business promotion, sporting events, and education unrelated to religion. Religion shall be private, not public. Members of a religion group shall not wear any article of clothing or emblem in public to identify a religious group. This would split society into an in-group and an out-group.

Blending of religion

Although religious diversity may initially present some problems, the outlook is promising. Religions are typically associated with specific racial/ethnic groups. As the racial and ethnic groups inter-marry, the religions will also merge. Catholics will marry Moslems; Protestants will marry Buddhists. All the major religions have much in common; their code of ethics is very similar even though doctrine may differ. The long term trend is toward ecumenism, to draw together and project a sense of unity and common direction.

Uniworld will encourage different religious groups to share a common house of prayer, used by each on a pre-arranged schedule, and sometimes jointly. This is more efficient and less wasteful than if each has its own church or temple. Religious services and religious education programs will also be on television and the Uninet.

An important cultural change that will materially facilitate religious blending is that children will not automatically follow the religion of their parents. Children will be exposed to the teachings of many religions and will be free to choose which, if any, they choose to adopt.

A Parliament of Religions will be set up in every region of the world, comprising representatives of every religion, and a world-wide Parliament of Religions, that would convene periodically. The purpose is to discuss issues that relate to religion, to resolve inter-religion problems, and to foster a spirit of respect for and cooperation among all religions.

Discrimination

People might differ in many ways: gender, race, skin color, ethnicity, age, height, fat/thin, religion, sexual orientation, and many other. Any difference that distinguishes one group of persons from another might lead to discrimination. Usually it's an external physical characteristic that is readily observed, but some - religious affiliation for example - may not be apparent unless identified by a special article of clothing.

Discrimination implies that certain groups are assigned an inferior status with fewer economic or social privileges. A society may have many different identifiable groups but if they are all treated equally there is no discrimination. If there is discrimination the dominant group will be the larger and more powerful.

Discrimination will be virtually a non-problem in Uniworld. All the racial and ethnic groups will merge so every one now has similar skin color and similar physical appearance. This still leaves gender and religion as a possible source of discrimination. As mentioned previously the primary cause of discrimination is economic competition, especially for jobs. But in Uniworld everyone has a guaranteed living income, job shortage is not a problem, and hence little reason for gender or religious discrimination.

In the Western World, women have made great progress toward

gender equality in recent years, but in many Third World countries women still have a very inferior status. Discrimination against homosexuals has also decreased in recent years. There are some indication that homosexual orientation might have a genetic basis; if so, it might be redirected genetically in the future.

Religious discrimination remains a possible problem, even though the various religions have much in common. As ethnic and racial groups merge, their religions will also blend.

Uniworld will also avoid discrimination based on geographic region of residence. All regions of the world will speak the same language, be the same ethnicity, have similar standard of living, education, and cultural opportunities. But to reduce the risk of development of insularity, everyone will be given the opportunity and encouraged to live in two or three different parts of the world during his lifetime. Geographic mobility was discussed in Chapter 6.

CHAPTER TEN
SOCIAL PROBLEMS

Some of the social problems of today's world, such as unemployment and poverty, will be resolved in Uniworld, but many other problems, such as crime and drugs, will still be with us. However Uniworld will be able to cope much better with these carryover problems.

Crime

Today the cost of crime is tremendous and getting worse. Uniworld is not a perfect society and will not be crime-free, but crime will be substantially lower.

Poverty is a principal reason for property-related crime such as robbery, theft, and burglary. If you are without a job and unable to buy the necessities of living, or feed a drug addiction, theft might appear to be a viable option. But in Uniworld drug addiction will be greatly reduced and everyone will have a guaranteed income sufficient to provide basic needs. You don't need to steal.

We also have white-collar crimes such as embezzlement, insurance fraud, arson, counterfeit products. These will still be with us in Uniworld but much less frequent.

In addition to crimes motivated by monetary gain, we will have "crimes of passion" - violence, aggression, rape, child abuse, spousal abuse, and similar. Unless we are willing to turn everyone into emotionless automatons these crimes will continue. But Uniworld will be a "kinder and gentler" society, with much less violence. Often aggression and family abuse is an outlet for frustrations of economic insecurity. In Uniworld everyone will have economic security.

Guns

The gun lobby has enshrined the right of each of us to own a gun as a holy privilege - the 11th commandment to supplement the original Ten Commandments. With heartfelt emotion they refer to the second amendment to the US Constitution:

"A well-regulated militia, being necessary to the security of a free

State, the right of the people to keep and bear arms, shall not be infringed."

This amendment was one of the first 10 amendments to the US Constitution, usually referred to as the Bill of Rights, adopted shortly after the Constitution was ratified. The United States was created by a federation of 13 independent states, giving up sovereignty with much reluctance and trepidation. Many were fearful that a strong central government might abuse its power. The Bill of Rights, including the right of private citizens to own arms, was a means of easing such fears. If the central government ill-used its authority, the private citizens, with arms they already owned, could overthrow the government.

The crazy militia groups, scattered around our country, still think this way, but most of us do not believe we need to arm ourselves for the impending overthrow of the government. Because of the huge and worsening problem of violent crime, many otherwise rational people believe everyone should have the right to own a gun for personal protection. If gun ownership is banned, law-abiding citizens will observe the law, but the criminals will not. The end result will be a general public unarmed and defenseless against criminals with automatic firearms.

We now have in America a nation with millions of gun owners and over 40,000 deaths per year from firearms. Many of the deaths are family disputes that escalated out of control. Gun-shot injuries cost the nation $40 billion a year.

Uniworld will ban the ownership of guns by the general public. The manufacture of guns and ammunition will be forbidden, except for a small government-operated facility, to equip police departments. The small quantity of guns owned by police departments would be held in reserve for special emergencies only, not for regular law enforcement. It is possible a criminal group might set up a hidden facility to manufacture guns. In such a case the police could draw on its reserve supply of weapons and take appropriate action.

Hunting rifles? Not permitted; if allowed they would become the weapon of choice for criminals. Though not as convenient to carry or to conceal, rifles can be modified for criminal use. The assassin of

President Kennedy used a rifle. Many law-abiding citizens enjoy hunting, but the restriction is necessary. Instead these hunters will hunt with a camera.

Some critics will point out that hunting is needed to limit the size of the game herd. Without hunting, the game population will grow beyond what the available food supply can support, and many will starve. It is more humane to cull the herd by controlled hunting. In earlier times however the working of natural law kept the size of the herd in check without the assistance of Man.

Alcoholic beverages

Alcoholism affects 14% of all adults and at least 100,000 deaths each year in the United States alone are associated with alcohol abuse. A recent government report estimates the yearly cost of alcoholism at $98.6 billion. The National Public Research Institute estimates alcoholism costs the nation $128 billion a year (the equivalent of 50 cents per drink).

Alcohol is a valuable industrial chemical. It is an important fuel, an ingredient in the manufacture of many chemical products, and also has many uses in medicine. As a beverage in moderation it has appeal. A glass of wine with dinner is one of life's pleasures, and is reported to be beneficial for the heart.

But consumption of excess quantities can have disastrous effects. For many people alcohol is highly addictive resulting in alcoholism, often the root cause of child abuse and spousal abuse. Many alcoholics become completely dysfunctional, unable to hold a job, and the family is added to the public welfare roll. Health is destroyed, and the alcoholic becomes a drain on the health care system.

The most serious downside of alcoholism is drunken driving causing over 40,000 deaths per year in the United States alone, and many more serious injuries. The economic cost of drunken driving is tremendous: loss of lives, medical treatment of the injured, cost of repairs to vehicles and other property, broken homes, cost of litigation, police department cost, and pain and suffering.

Ideally we'd like to have a two-tier system: those that will drink moderately are permitted to buy and use alcohol, while those at risk of drinking to excess, will not be permitted to buy and use alcohol. But this is not a feasible system. How do we know who are moderate drinkers and who are not except by hindsight? How could we ever police such a system? Either we permit alcohol or we prohibit it.

In 1917 the Congress of the United States passed the infamous 18th amendment to the Constitution prohibiting the manufacture and sale of "intoxicating liquors". It went into effect January 1919 after ratification by the states but it was never very effective. Bootleg whiskey took the place of whiskey from legitimate distillers, speakeasies took the place of neighborhood bars, and the economy minded made bathtub gin. The public did not support this law. Along with the high cost of efforts to enforce prohibition we had police corruption and a breakdown of public respect for the law. Finally in February 1933 Congress passed the 21st Amendment to the Constitution repealing the 18th Amendment. This was ratified by the states December 1933 and the noble experiment ended.

Currently some of the states in India have initiated prohibition of liquor. It was the women who pressed aggressively for enactment. Getting drunk is a common way for the men of the village to end the day after work. This frequently leads to wife-beating when she prefers to use the small earnings of the husband for food for the family rather than for liquor. But the results have been similar to our experience - bootleg whiskey of doubtful quality at a high price and police corruption. Moreover the state has lost the second-largest source of tax revenue; schools and health care has suffered.

Uniworld would prefer to prohibit alcohol - the downside far outweighs the advantages - but it will be difficult to enforce. A compromise approach is to permit beer and light wines but no hard liquors. Restaurant and bars may sell only one serving of an alcoholic beverage to a patron. Uniworld will have severe penalties for drunk driving and schools will teach dangers of alcoholism. Alcoholic beverages will be subject to heavy sales tax and advertising will not be permitted.

Cigarettes

Cigarettes have few redeeming features. Alcoholics harm not only themselves, but also their family and the victims of auto accidents they cause. Except for second hand smoke, cigarette users primarily harm themselves.

There is no evidence that cigarettes fill a basic human craving. However smoking is highly addictive, and for some users, the craving is almost irresistible. You will not become addicted to cigarettes if you never smoke.

Cigarette smoking carries a heavy economic burden. Primarily it greatly increases the risk of lung cancer and other respiratory illnesses, and this is reflected in higher health care costs. The thousands of persons employed in the tobacco industry are making a product that is worse than useless; it is harmful. The industry is also consuming energy and creating waste that must be disposed of.

Uniworld will prohibit the growing of tobacco, and the manufacture and sale of cigarettes.

Narcotic Drugs

Drug abuse, according to the National Public Research Institute, costs the United States $122 billion a year.

Opium, grown around the world, is derived from the juice of poppy plants; morphine is extracted from opium, and heroin is extracted from morphine. Heroin, a highly addictive substance, has been deemed "the greatest public health hazard" by the United Nations. Cocaine, extracted from a shrub grown in South America, can be snorted or injected. In crystalline form, known as "crack", it is smoked. The annual income of crime syndicates involved in the drug trade is estimated at $750 billion.

We are not born with a need for narcotic drugs, but once we start using them, most of us will become addicted and many will end up with destroyed lives. Because of the harm of drug addiction, the government has made illegal the production, sale, and possession of narcotic drugs. Similar to the previous prohibition of alcohol, anti-drug legislation has driven the drug trade underground. The price of drugs has risen sharply and concurrently so have drug trade profits. Attempts to enforce the law have cost hundreds of millions of dollars with little success. Thousand of young persons, primarily in the inner cities, have joined gangs, such as the Crips, the Bloods, the 18th Street gang, whose primary activity is the drug trade.

Frustrated by the failure of enforcement, it has been proposed that drugs be made legal. Users will come out of hiding and be more willing to undergo treatment to break the addiction. The price of drugs will drop substantially, the drug trade profits will drop, and some of the drug-lords may even quit the drug trade.

Others oppose legalizing drugs. If drugs are legal it will remove the stigma of drug use. Many young people will assume if the government permits it, it must be harmless. At a reduced price many will try it simply out of curiosity and then get hooked.

Uniworld will ban narcotic drugs, except for medical use when prescribed by a physician. These drugs have been found useful in pain relief for cancer patients and when so used rarely causes addiction. Of course if the patient is terminally ill, addiction is irrelevant.

Gambling

Though less serious than alcohol and narcotic drugs, gambling is another problem area. It gives the wrong message to young people: we get ahead by luck. The better message for success is: a good education and hard work.

A bet in the state-run lottery is a foolish gamble. Typically 25% of the bet goes for overhead, 25% to the state, and the remaining 50% is paid back to the bettors. Thus you automatically lose 50% on average. Actually the loss is much more than 50% since the jackpot is paid to the winner over a 20 year period. A $1,000,000 winner receives $50,000 a year for 20 years. At a 10% interest rate, the present value of $50,000 a year for 20 years is only $426,000, not $1,000,000 so in effect the lottery players get back less than 25%. This is a huge "house" cut. The casinos in Las Vegas make handsome profits on a house edge of less than 5%.

The rationale for the state run lottery is that the state profit is earmarked for education. But the tax money allocated to education is reduced by a corresponding amount, so in reality the lottery profit goes into general state revenue. The state does make some money, but most of it comes from low income lottery players. There are better ways to generate revenue for the state. And 25% of the ticket revenue goes to the private company that runs the lottery for the state, a complete waste.

Gambling does have at least one redeeming feature - it can be exciting and fun. Poker without betting doesn't make sense. Uniworld will allow small scale betting - primarily on sporting events such as horse races and football games. The total amount of money you may bet in one day, one month, and one year will be limited. Gambling is to be a recreational activity and is not to become a way of life. For some persons, gambling is a serious addiction, wasting much of their income, and ending in financial ruin for their families. Gamblers Anonymous help groups have been set up similar to Alcoholics Anonymous. Many of us must be protected from our own folly.

Treating addiction

Alcoholism, smoking, drugs, and compulsive gambling are all forms of addiction. According to a recent article in Newsweek (5/5/97) some scientists believe these addictions share a common mechanism, the amount of dopamine in the brain. Dopamine is a neuro-transmitter that connects the signals from one neuron to another and is associated with a feeling of euphoria. Dopamine output can be increased by pleasant experiences, by an enjoyable meal, by sex, but also by drugs. For example, amphetamine stimulates the dopamine-producing cells to increase their output. Due to a genetic disorder, some persons do not have an adequate release of dopamine in normal life experiences, and these persons are more likely to turn to drugs to overcome the deficiency.

According to this theory, drug addiction has a biological basis, and is a form of mental illness. Drug abuse in the U.S. is said to have a medical and social cost of more than $240 billion a year. We spend $10 billion a year trying to enforce anti-drug laws, but only $5 billion a year on prevention and treatment.

Meanwhile there have been some recent developments. According to a report in Newsweek (1/30/95) experiments are underway in Spain, Israel, and Mexico to treat heroin addicts with naltrexone. a narcotic antagonist that binds to the receptors in the brain more strongly than heroin or cocaine and displaces them. Because the withdrawal effect is so traumatic, in some treatment centers the addict is anesthetized for six to eight hours during the detoxification stage. It is a dangerous treatment, monitored by physicians, with patient under heavy sedation in an intensive-care unit. Purpose of the treatment is to induce ultra-rapid detoxification. Instead of shaking, sweating, and retching 10 days or more, the patient purportedly goes home clean after a brief hospital stay. This is not a magical cure; long term follow up still is necessary. Naltrexone is also showing promise in reducing craving for alcohol when combined with psychotherapy.

The most common treatment today for heroin addiction is methadone. This is a powerful analgesic that acts like an opiate in the body but without producing euphoria and blocks the addict's craving for heroin. Some critics however contend that methadone merely substitutes one addiction for another.

Since it is widely believed that drug addiction has a biological and genetic basis, resulting in a type of mental disorder, Uniworld will focus actively on research to develop the most effective methods to prevent and combat all forms of addictions. Within the next 20-30 years it is reasonable to expect substantial progress.

Enforcement

As discussed above, Uniworld will ban guns, hard liquor, cigarettes, narcotic drugs (except for medical use), and will take strong steps to reduce all criminal activity.

The primary motivation for property crime and for the manufacture and sale of illegal substances is profit. Enforcement will be much more effective in Uniworld because of the cash-less monetary system. Every money transfer is recorded on the Uninet, the world-wide computer network, leaving a transaction record that is readily traced. Uniworld will still have petty theft, such as stealing a TV for personal use, but if you steal 100 TV's, how will you sell them?

Criminals of course can circumvent the record trail of the cash-less monetary system by setting up a off-record barter system. A crime-organized barter system might be feasible on a small scale, but a large operation would be difficult to conceal.

In the movies, the jewel thieves, after successfully completing the multi-million heist, escape to Brazil or some far off land with the loot. The next scene shows them lounging on the beach, safe from extradition. enjoying their newly-acquired wealth. In Uniworld, a world government, they would need to escape to Mars to be safe from extradition, and maybe not even safe there.

In Uniworld the police will be able to quickly trace the whereabouts of a criminal suspect. Every infant at birth is implanted with an Embedded Identification Chip (EIC). If a person is suspected of a crime, the police, after first securing a court order, can remotely activate circuitry in the EIC so that the location of the suspect is readily detected.

Prisons and capital punishment

Prison operation is a heavy economic burden on society, and is increasingly so, with the get-tough-on-crime political mood and tough laws such as California's "three strikes, you're out". Many young criminals are being sentenced to life terms without parole. We will need to support them for perhaps 70 years at an annual cost in excess of $30,000 per year. And as these young prison inmates become old prison inmates, we will have the additional burden of providing costly medical care.

In Uniworld prison inmates will work at productive jobs, similar to work outside of prisons. Today, inmates are primarily poor, ill-educated minorities from dysfunctional homes. In Uniworld, prisoners will differ little from the general population. Because of ethnic blending, there will be no minorities, they will come from average middle-class families, will have good education, mostly including two years of college, and capable of productive work.

Some prisons will have their own industrial plants, but most low-risk inmates will work outside the prison in regular jobs, alongside non-inmates. At the end of the workday they will return to prison and remain there until the next workday. Their Embedded Identification Chip (EIC) will be activated so their whereabouts is readily traced.

These prison inmates will earn a normal salary, according to the work they do, but the entire salary, except for a special reserve, is paid to the prison to cover the expense of prison operation. Some of the younger inmates, because of limited work experience, may earn only $2,000 a month, while others may earn $5,000 a month and higher, but regardless, the entire amount is paid to the prison, except for the reserve.

Part of the reserve is available to the inmate for certain personal expenses - books, toothpaste, etc. Balance of the reserve is placed in a special savings account which is released when sentence is completed. If the inmate has a family or other dependents, part of the earnings will go directly to the dependents.

If the inmate refuses to work, he will not be forced to work, but incentives and disincentives will make it advantageous to work. If he doesn't work he will lose certain privileges, his sentence will be longer, his dependents will have less income, and he won't receive the accumulated savings account.

Because prison inmates work and their job income mostly is paid to the prison to cover the costs of prison operation, the prison system is a much less economic burden on Uniworld than our present system. The Uniworld system of working inmates can not be used today, because labor unions would object to the job competition. In Uniworld, there is no unemployment; everyone available for work has a job. The Uniworld system of working inmates also somewhat resolves the question of capital punishment. Some crimes are so brutal, so vicious, justice almost cries out for capital punishment. The only alternate is life imprisonment without parole, but this puts an economic burden of perhaps several million dollars to house this criminal for the next 50-70 years. From this point of view, capital punishment saves tax dollars. But if the criminal is working, the economic burden is minimized, one less reason to justify capital punishment.

Although the purpose of the prison system is to punish anti-social behavior, to act as a deterrent to others, and to isolate dangerous criminals from society, Uniworld will also emphasize rehabilitation of first-time offenders and will do extensive research to develop effective methods of rehabilitation, without resorting to mind control and brain washing.

CHAPTER ELEVEN
LIFE IN UNIWORLD

Life style in Uniworld will not differ radically from what we have in today's world.

Political structure

The political structure in Uniworld will be similar to what we presently have in the United States: a representative democracy with three branches of government - legislative, executive, and judicial.

Uniworld will have 20,000 cities of 100,000 each. A metropolitan area consists of a cluster of five cities, a combined population of 500,000. Ten metropolitan areas, located in close proximity, will comprise a Region, a combined population of 5 million. Thus the entire world will be divided into 400 Regions.

Each metropolitan 5-city area will have a local government with administrative functions, elected by popular vote, and a judicial system. To avoid politicizing the judiciary, judges will be appointed, rather than elected. Each metro-area will elect one representative to the Region's judicial committee. This committee of ten will appoint the judges in each metro-area. Each Region will also elect by popular vote one representative to the Uniworld Congress.

To maintain a uniform civil and criminal code throughout the world, all the laws will be made by the Uniworld Congress. Local officials in the metropolitan areas administer the law, but do not create their own laws. They are empowered however to enact local ordinances.

The Uniworld Congress, consisting of 400 members, will be in session much less frequently than the present US Congress. Many of the concerns that occupy Congress now will no longer be a factor in Uniworld - foreign affairs, defense budget, balance of trade, foreign exchange, welfare, affirmative action, highway expansion, immigration, terrorism, nuclear proliferation, and others. Once Uniworld passes through the very difficult transition period, which will take 100-200 years, Uniworld will be a very stable society. However nothing remains unchanged forever; problems will arise and adjustments must be made and the Uniworld Congress will need to respond appropriately.

Marriage and family

Every young adult will have a detailed genetic profile. A couple contemplating marriage is required to first meet with a genetic counselor. The purpose is to evaluate the probability the couple will have healthy children. The goal is not to breed super-child, but to reduce the risk of bearing children with serious physical or mental disabilities.

In some cases the risk can be minimized by genetic techniques. Another possibility is to fertilize the egg in vitro, screen it, and implant it in the womb only if it appears to be normal. In some cases, the risk can be avoided only if each marries a different partner. If the couple still wants to marry, they must agree to be childless.

Most families will have two children; some will have three. During the transition period in which the world population is to be reduced to two billion, the average family will have just one child. But once we near the two billion population goal, we will encourage the two child family. For a stable population, birth rate needs to be 2.1 children per couple, so some families will have three children. Birth rate in the western countries today is less than 1.7; in the Third World countries it is much higher. As Uniworld goes into effect, as women become more empowered, birthrate in the Third World will decline substantially.

Uniworld is not anti-children; to the contrary, Uniworld subsidizes children. A family with children under 18 years of age will receive social security benefits for each child and for a non-working spouse.

Divorce and children

Divorce has high emotional and economic cost to the couple involved and to society as a whole, especially if the disrupted family includes young children. About half of all marriages in the United States end in divorce. Easier "no-fault" divorce, reduced religious influence, and greater economic independence of women, have all increased the frequency of divorce.

Uniworld will not restrict divorce but does prefer fewer divorces. If a couple can not get along, and the differences are irreconcilable, divorce is usually better than an unworkable marriage, even if children are involved.

The practical goal is few divorces. Every high school will include a course relating to marriage and the family - finding a mate, sex, children, and financial management. Marriage counselors will be available for consultation, at no cost or small cost, for married and single persons, as part of the universal health care system.

In addition to conferring with a genetic counselor, a prospective couple, before marriage, will also be required to confer with a marriage counselor that will evaluate the likelihood of a successful marriage. If the counselor's report is unfavorable, the marriage must be postponed 6 months, at which time there will be another evaluation conference. The couple is then free to go ahead with the marriage, even if the second report is again negative. However many couples, confronted with a pessimistic opinion, may decide against marriage.

Divorce is much less traumatic if no children are involved. The greatest risk of divorce is during the first few years of marriage. With this in mind, a couple is not permitted to start a pregnancy during the first 12 months of marriage, and is encouraged to wait 2 years. As an essential part of the limitation of population growth, every adult of child-propagating age is inoculated with a long-term birth-control drug. The drug that will neutralize the birth-control drug and restore fertility is available only at a government clinic.

The 12 month waiting period without children is a valuable trial period. After one year the couple can elect to start a family. However they must first confer with a marriage counselor who makes an evaluation for their consideration, but regardless of the evaluation, the couple has the right then to start a family.

Money problem is frequently the root cause of marital discord. The Uniworld family, with guaranteed income and -universal health care, will rarely have a major money problem, so it is expected Uniworld will have a much lower divorce rate than we have now.

Teen-age sex

Teen-age sex is a major social issue. In some US cities today half the pregnancies are to teen-age girls. Children of teen-age mothers are at great risk of poverty, crime, homelessness, drugs, school dropout. Teen-age sex is usually unprotected sex with high frequency of sexually-transmitted disease (STD).There are practically no positive elements to teen-age out-of-wedlock parenting, and determined efforts must be made to prevent it.

It is unrealistic to prohibit teen-age sex. In earlier times puberty began about age 15-16, especially in colder climates, but now many children are sexually mature as young as 11 years of age and it is difficult to deny the libido. They are still children but unfortunately are already physically capable of having babies. We must do our best to discourage teen age pregnancies by aggressive education campaigns to induce all sexually-active youths to use contraception, provided free or at small charge. These contraceptive methods should be designed to also protect against the transmission of AIDS and other sexual diseases.

Education unfortunately is not always effective. Some youths lack self-discipline, some are careless, and some just don't care. Perhaps more can be done, such as:

a. Sex before age 20 is illegal.

b. Compulsory abortion of teen-age pregnancies.

c. Genetic engineering that delays sexual maturity until age 20.

d. An implant injected into every child at age 10 that delays sexual maturity until age 20.

e. An implant injected into every child at age 10 that prevents conception for 10 years.

f. Virtual reality sex without physical contact prior to age 20.

None of these are ideal solutions. Prohibition of teen-age sex would be impossible to enforce. Compulsory abortion would be violently opposed as a violation of religious freedom and civil liberties. To delay sexual maturity or fertility until age 20 genetically or by an implant is possibly acceptable, if effective, safe, and without harmful side effects. We have no such genetic or medical capability yet, but this is a worthwhile area for future research.

The desire for sex is inherent in human nature, as in all living creatures; if sex was not pleasurable, the human race would not have survived. Sex is one of life's wonderful experiences, but it can be misused. It is not feasible, and probably not even desirable, to prohibit teen-age sex, but it must be properly directed.

One acceptable method of sexual expression is masturbation, self-generated sex without a partner. The word "masturbation" is somewhat uncomfortable, and rarely spoken in polite society; perhaps we should refer to it as "mono-sex" instead. We need somewhat of a change in cultural attitudes to view mono-sex as a normal expression of sexuality, and not an immoral embarrassment. Especially for teen-agers it is preferable to sexually-transmitted diseases and unwanted pregnancies.

Mono-sex can be enhanced by mechanical devices such as vibrators and vacuum pumps, along with visual and auditory stimulation provided by specially prepared video tapes and CD-ROMs.

A more elaborate form of mono-sex is virtual reality sex using computer simulation with a fictitious partner, or a partner on the Uninet, or the actual person the teen-ager is dating. The computers used might be home equipment, but for the most complete experience, the young couple will go to a special computer-equipped facility, similar to those used for high-tech video games or flight simulation. The boy and girl each go into a separate room. The computer program simulates the complete sex act, including visual and tactile enhancement, without the risk of pregnancy or disease.

Virtual reality sex might be a very effective substitute for the real thing but many will still prefer real sex. A carrot-stick approach might help; penalties and loss of privileges for those that have real sex; special preferences for those that wait until marriage.

The sex-related problems of disease, especially AIDS, and unwanted pregnancies, apply not only to teen-agers but also to unmarried adults. For these persons also, mono-sex and virtual reality sex will be encouraged as a preferable substitute for actual sexual intercourse. For married couples in a monogamous relationship no substitute is needed. Perhaps this compensates for the marriage penalty in the income tax code.

Education

Uniworld will provide free public education for every child from kindergarten through two years of junior college. In addition to the standard core subjects of language, math, history, and science, the curriculum will regularly include consumer education, money management, ethics, sex education, human relations, and current affairs.

Note the inclusion of ethics. We can no longer depend entirely upon religion and the home to instill ethical concepts. We have a near-crisis in ethics today. According to a recent study, 40% of high school students admit to having cheated on a test or shop-lifted during the prior 12 months. Over 50% would lie on a resume if it would help get a better job. It doesn't matter whether it's right or wrong, but only whether or not you can get away with it.

Computers will be used extensively, but will supplement and not replace, live teachers. Every student will also have access to a computer at home, and they will be as common as the TV set.

Tuition at the most prestigious universities can cost in excess of $15,000 a year, plus living expenses. In the future many college students will take their courses on the computer network, rather than in residence, at a considerable saving, especially for courses that are primarily reading and lectures. Group discussions will be held periodically by teleconferencing.

However some fields of study such as engineering and medicine, require hands-on instruction, but even some of these fields include lecture courses, which can be taught effectively over the computer network.

Charities

Today we have thousands of charitable and non-profit institutions, such as Harvard University, City of Hope Medical Center, Salvation Army, American Cancer Society, Wilderness Society, United Nations

Association, United Way.

Some of the charity programs will no longer be needed; for example, those that assist the poor. With universal health care and social security, poverty will be rare. Hopefully we will have no need for organizations that advocate population limits and protection of the environment; this will all be part of basic government policy.

Hospitals will be supported by the universal health care system, which will reimburse the hospital for services performed, and to a lesser extent by patient co-payments. Medical and scientific research will be financed by the government directly through a government agency or by a grant.

The disadvantage of the present private-financed charities is that so much of their time and effort is needed in fund raising. In many cases, as much as l/3rd of their operating expenses is used in fund solicitation.

Another disadvantage is that charities compete with each other for funds, and some worthy organizations do not survive. It is not always survival of the fittest and the best, but rather survival of those that are best at raising money. Furthermore the funds raised are often disproportionate to the importance or scope of the program. A minor program that has emotional appeal may raise more money than a major program that is more difficult to market.

To replace private charities by government-financed programs may appear to be a dubious improvement. The government is not always noted for efficient management, but it should work out. First, there will be an oversight committee that will continually review and monitor these programs and make appropriate changes. Second, we are saving the cost of fund-raising, probably at least 20%, so if the government is no more than 20% less efficient than private charities, the cost comparison is break-even. Third, the funds can be allocated more efficiently to the diverse programs than if left to private contributors that lack the time and information to make such decisions. Fourth, Uniworld will be a very stable society and the needs these programs are directed toward will continue with limited change year after year. So even if the government is less than efficient at the start, it is not chasing a continually moving target, and efficiency will improve in time.

Leisure

An efficient economy can provide a good standard of living, but we are adding another goal - a good quality of life. This requires the satisfying use of the expanded leisure time that Uniworld will provide to all adults, something better than 5 hours daily before the TV set.

For many retired persons today the principal activity is the daily trip to the doctor. In the future in Uniworld with advances in medical treatment retired people will be healthier and more active. Those still in the workforce will enjoy a shorter workweek, due to a more efficient economy, higher productivity, and the decline of consumerism.

Once the Uniworld economy is well established, the work week will gradually decline from 40 hours a week, to 35 hours, to 30 hours, and even less. As discussed in a prior chapter, a basic principal of the Uniworld economy is anti-consumerism. "If you don't need it, don't buy it".

Assume the work week has been reduced, by gains in productivity, from 40 hours previously down to 30 hours, and this is still sufficient to provide everyone with an adequate standard of living. Everyone now has an additional 10 hours a week of leisure. However some may suggest that, instead of 10 hours more leisure, let's increase the work week and produce more luxury goods.

Uniworld will resist the shift towards consumerism. Even though we have the manpower available to produce luxuries, such production consumes raw material and energy, has negative impact on the environment, and adds to problems of waste disposal. Uniworld's goal is a satisfying life, and this should not depend on unnecessary material consumption. A far better use of the shorter work week is the opportunity for increased leisure.

Leisure can be used for recreation, for volunteer work, and for personal development.

Recreation includes travel, spectator sports, theater, concerts, bridge, chess, social dancing, reading, and yes, watching TV. Neighborhood community centers will provide recreation in the form of team sports for different skill levels, with emphasis on participation rather than on winning.

Even though charities in Uniworld will be government funded, the charities will be staffed primarily by volunteers with compassion that are willing to provide a community service. Retired persons in good health will be encouraged to volunteer to assist patients at home, in hospitals, and in nursing homes. Volunteers will be used in medical research, in environmental protection programs, to assist students with learning disabilities, and in many other community programs.

Personal development is a third way to use leisure time. This includes;

a. adult education
b. the arts: painting, sculpting, drama, writing, singing, music, etc.
c. craft skills: cabinetry, model building, dress design, pottery, etc.
e. physical fitness: fitness classes, walking, running, golf, tennis, soccer, etc.

Uniworld will strongly encourage lifelong learning for adults. Some programs will be work and career oriented to improve work capability; others will be only enrichment courses that have no monetary advantage but improve quality of life - literature, history, art, astronomy, philosophy, the natural sciences, and others. Courses for adults will be given in public schools, junior colleges, community centers, and increasingly at home over the Uninet.

Some of these programs will be provided for a fee by for-profit businesses, but most will be provided, at no charge or nominal charge, at neighborhood community centers, a basic component of all cities. Volunteers, by personal home visits, will encourage everyone to participate within their physical limitations. Too often we don't know a neighbor just two doors away. These group activities will bring people together, creating a valuable sense of community.

Uniworld will make available a great variety of leisure activities, but participation is not compulsory. Some people just want to be let alone, and that is acceptable, but most people will welcome the opportunity.

It is a human trait that many of us are encouraged to participate if there is a measure of achievement and some form of recognition for achievement. The merit badge program of the Boy Scouts is a possible approach. The Boy Scouts award a merit badge when a course of study and a project is completed in subjects such as first aid, astronomy, music, bird study, cabinet making, photography, and dozens of others. In a similar way we can set up standard courses on a great variety of subjects, at different levels, with a specified point value assigned to each relative to difficulty and estimated time required. A silver personal achievement pin is earned for 1,000 accumulated points, a gold pin for 5,000 points, and is awarded in a special annual community ceremony.

Volunteer work is similarly recognized. One point is earned for every volunteer work hour. A silver volunteer pin is earned for 1,000 volunteer hours, a gold pin for 5,000 hours, and is awarded in a special ceremony.

The wise use of leisure time will enrich the lives of everyone and will make retirement truly the golden years.

CHAPTER TWELVE
SUMMARY AND CONCLUSIONS

What Do You Suggest?

Let us assume you agree the present trend of world society is heading for disaster. With a quick reading of the Uniworld Plan, you may concede that it may have some merit, but is the Uniworld Plan the best solution? This may be acceptable for a first effort, but certainly there may be other and better possibilities. Let's consider this.

The heart of the Uniworld Plan is a world government, a stable world population of two billion, and a protected environment. Our goal is a good standard of living for everyone and this requires a worldwide plan and that requires a world government. It may be a theoretical possibility, but not a practical possibility, to accomplish this with 185 sovereign nations each determined to protect its perceived national interests. What do you suggest?

We can't provide a good standard of living for everyone now, and certainly not for future generations, if we destroy our environmental capital, our resource base. Unless we take active steps to limit population, it will continue to grow to 10 billion, to 14 billion, and more. You may say that population will eventually level off if we leave it alone. That is true - it will eventually level off - when the environment is destroyed and half the world is starving and the other half is desperately trying to protect their limited food supply from seizure. This is nature's way; when the number of animals exceed the number the food supply can support, the surplus starve until a new balance is reached. But mankind is supposedly superior to animals; man is able to foresee a future problem and take corrective steps in advance. What do you suggest?

Our present population nearing 6 billion is not sustainable; it must be reduced. The Uniworld Plan calls for a population of two billion. Why not three billion? There is nothing sacred about two billion. This was world population in 1930 and it appears to be a practical number. Maybe three billion is sustainable. As the population is being reduced from its starting level, it will come down to 3 billion before it reaches 2 billion. The decision can be made then whether further reduction down to 2 billion is needed. If any doubt, the 2 billion level provides a margin of safety. Whether the proper level is 2 billion or 3 billion may be open to discussion, but there is no question that 10 billion is not sustainable. What do you suggest?

The Uniworld economy is a free market economy directed towards providing basic goods and services with maximum efficiency and minimum waste. Luxury products are permitted but are discouraged by a graduated sales tax. What do you suggest?

Uniworld will have a cash-less monetary system. This is the trend, with or without Uniworld.

Uniworld will have a common language and the blending of all racial and ethnic groups into a universal humanity. A thousand years ago hundreds of different languages and diverse ethnic groups developed naturally by physical isolation, but today with greater freedom of movement and of communication, in the absence of political and economic restraints, diverse groups will mix and inter-marry and differences will disappear. Uniworld will simply encourage the acceleration of this natural trend. What do you suggest?

Uniworld will have a government sponsored universal social security system and universal health insurance. You probably agree with the purpose, but you may believe it would more efficient if in the private sector. Private plans will offer greater flexibility of choice but has the disadvantage that some people will be well-insured while others will fall between the cracks. A government plan is more democratic; it will cover everyone equally. Although a government plan may initially be inefficient, the cost will be lower than a for-profit private plan once the rough edges are smoothed. And Uniworld is better able to afford an adequate plan, government or private, because a world government is spared the heavy expense of supporting a military force and the cost of war. What do you suggest?

Uniworld will have cities of 100,000 standard size in which most people can walk or bike to work, school, or shopping. This is feasible with a world population of two billion. If 15 billion population, it would require 150,000 separate cities. There are nowhere near enough suitable locations for that many separate cities. Do you suggest cities of one million each? That would require "only" 15,000 sites.

The Uniworld Plan covers an extensive number of topics in addition to the ones discussed above. These other topics in general are important but not as basic. For some of these you may very well have a proposal that is better than what is proposed here. Your suggestions are welcome.

Why can't the First World go it alone?

Some readers may agree with much of the Uniworld plan - population limits, protection of the environment, and other features - but question the feasibility of making it a world wide project, including sub-Saharan Africa, Bangladesh, and the rest of the Third World. Certainly it would be much easier for the First World to achieve the Uniworld goals on its own.

Yes, it would be much, much easier if the First World could go it alone, and not have to worry about the rest of the world. Easier, yes; possible, no. There are several reasons why the First World can't go it alone. First, we depend on certain resources that are found only in the Third World. Second, we will be unable to stop global warming, destruction of the ozone layer, and pollution of the water and air, and possibly even nuclear war in the Third World, all of which is disastrous for everyone. Third, there is the moral element. How can we stand by as spectators to the starvation and misery of the Third World knowing it might have been avoided if we had been willing to make some sacrifices? Fourth, terrorism. The Third World won't let us sit peacefully on the sidelines; they will take us down with them.

To illustrate this, let's quote some excerpts from Edgar Allan Poe's short story "The Masque of the Red Death":

"The "Red Death" had long devastated the country. No pestilence had ever been so fatal, or so hideous. Blood was its Avator and its seal - the redness and the horror of blood. There were sharp pains, and sudden dizziness, and then profuse bleeding at the pores, with dissolution. The scarlet stains upon the body and especially upon the face of the victim, were the pest ban which shut him out from the aid and from the sympathy of his fellowmen. And the whole seizure, progress, and termination of the disease, were the incidents of half an hour.

"But the Prince Prospero was happy and dauntless and sagacious. When his dominions were half depopulated, he summoned to his presence a thousand hale and lighthearted friends from among the knights and dames of his court, and with these retired to the deep seclusion of one of his castellated abbeys. This was an extensive and magnificent structure... A strong and lofty wall girded it in. This wall had gates of iron.

"The courtiers, having entered, brought furnaces and hammers and welded the bolts. They resolved to leave means neither of ingress nor egress to the sudden impulses of despair or of frenzy from within. The abbey was amply provisioned. With such precautions the courtiers might bid defiance to contagion. The external world could take care of itself. In the meantime it was folly to grieve, or to think. The prince had provided all the appliances of pleasure. There were buffoons, there were ballet dancers, there were musicians, there was Beauty, there was wine. All these and security were within. Without was the "Red Death".

"It was toward the fifth or sixth month of his seclusion, and while the pestilence raged most furiously abroad, that the Prince Prospero entertained his thousand friends at a masked ball of the most unusual magnificence... And the revel went whirlingly on, until at length there commenced the sounding of midnight upon the clock....Before the last echoes of the last chime had utterly sunk into silence, many individuals became aware of the presence of a masked figure which had arrested the attention of no single individual before... There arose at length from the whole company a murmur, expressive of disapprobation and surprise - then, finally of terror, or horror, and of disgust... It may well be supposed that no ordinary appearance could have excited such sensation, but the figure in question... had gone beyond the bounds of even the prince's indefinite decorum.

"The figure was tall and gaunt, and shrouded from head to foot in the habiliments of the grave. The mask... was made to resemble the countenance of a stiffened corpse... And yet all this might have been endured... but the mummer had gone so far as to assume the type of the "Red Death".

"When the eyes of Prince Prospero fell upon this spectral image, his brow reddened with rage. "Who dares" he demanded hoarsely " insult us with this blasphemous mockery. Seize him and unmask him"... there were found none who put forth hand to seize him.

"The intruder made his way, with deliberate and stately step, unimpeded... through the blue chamber to the purple - through the purple to the green - through the green to the orange - through this to the white - and then to the violet chamber. It was then, however, that the Prince Prospero, maddening with rage and the shame of his own momentary cowardice, rushed hurriedly through the six chambers.

"He bore aloft a drawn dagger, and had approached within three or four feet of the retreating figure, when the latter, turned suddenly and confronted his pursuer. There was a sharp cry, and the dagger dropped gleaming upon the sable carpet, upon which, instantly afterward, fell prostrate in death the Prince Prospero. Then, summoning the wild courage of despair, a throng of the revelers... seizing the mummer... gasped in unutterable horror at finding the grave cerements and corpse-like mask... untenanted by any tangible form.

"And now was acknowledged the presence of the Red Death. He had come like a thief in the night. And one by one dropped the revelers in the blood-bedewed halls of their revel, and died each in the despairing posture of his fall. And the flames of the tripods expired. And Darkness and Decay and the Red Death held illimitable dominion over all."

Question and Answers

Q. Why do we need a world government? A strengthened United Nations is more feasible and may work just as well?

A. A strengthened UN is a helpful first step, but only as a first step. We will be unable to accomplish our first essential goal - halt the population growth and then reduce the population to two billion persons - if we must depend on the voluntary cooperation of 185 independent nations. Time is working against us.

Q. Why two billion population? Why not stabilize at 6 billion, about where we are now?
A. Today the average American uses 23 times as much goods and services as the average Third Worlder. A population of 6 billion is not sustainable now, and will certainly not be sustainable once the Third World has an improved standard of living. Perhaps in the future we might be able to sustain a 3 billion population, but 2 billion gives us a safety margin.

Q. Your proposals for stopping population growth and reducing population to 2 billion are very coercive. Why not use education?
A. Education will be used in every possible way along with incentives, but we can't rely on voluntary cooperation alone. Here again, we don't have the time. We will need a one-child policy, and even if we were able to start at once, it will take at least 100 years to reduce world population to two billion. Most people will accept the one-child policy as necessary; some will resist it and for these regrettably it will be coercion. But the restriction is temporary. Once we reach the two billion population goal, most families will be able to have 2 children, and many 3 children.

Q. Why is it so important to try to reach the 2 billion goal in 100 years? If we moved more slowly many families could be permitted to have two children?
A. Our goal is a good standard of living for everyone and this requires a sustainable environment. Until we can reduce the population to 4 billion or less the environment is being seriously degraded. The longer we take to reduce the population the greater the harm to the environment and the slower the recovery.

Q. We may need a forum such as the United Nations to protect the environ-

ment, but we don't need a world government. The Earth Summit Rio de Janiero in 1992 made excellent progress.

A. Yes the Rio de Janiero meeting was an encouraging start but unfortunately the results have been disappointing. A special session of the United States was convened in June 1997 to review and appraise progress of the prior 5 years. According to Populations Communications International, the report indicates the environment is in worse condition than it was 5 years ago. Land degradation due to erosion, overgrazing, salinization, and alkalinization has put one billion persons in 110 countries at risk. In Africa, only 30% of virgin forest land is left. In Asia, timber reserves may last only another 40 years. Every day, 25,000 people die due to poor water quality. The risk of global warming is increasing; more and more carbon dioxide, from combustion of fossil fuels, is emitted into the atmosphere.

Q. Forty years ago it was estimated petroleum reserves would last only 40 years. Now we are still said to have a 40 year supply. Forty years from now, with improved technology for discovering and recovering oil, we will still have a 40 year reserve, with more oil yet to be discovered.

A. True, but eventually, whether 40 years or 140 years, we will exhaust all reserves that can be recovered at reasonable cost. Until then, we must use what we have wisely while we are developing a sustainable replacement.

Q. What other material shortages are likely?

A. Oil has been our major source of energy, but we will probably be able to replace it with solar energy. However oil as a chemical feed stock will be difficult to replace. Another long range problem will be finding a substitute for chromium, nickel, cobalt, manganese, tungsten, and other metals. When used these metals might oxidize or form other compounds but they are not destroyed. Theoretically they can be reprocessed, even though at high cost, and the metal recovered, but it is not possible to achieve 100% recovery. For example, a knife blade gradually wears out and there is no practical way to recover these microscopic particles.

Q. Arbitrarily limiting life span to an average of 80 years flies in the face of our inherent nature. Life span has been increasing steadily for the past 200 years and in another 100 years will possibly be 130 years or more. Why kill people before their time?

A. Yes, this a very controversial proposal that will meet with much resistance, but it is necessary. Sometimes the wish of the individual must yield to the needs of society. Perhaps medical science will be able to make some modification in our genes so that we no longer will want to live forever.

Q. You propose a controlled average life span of 80 years. Suppose future medical advances makes it possible for the average person to be active and healthy to 120 years. Would you then favor an increase to 120 years?

A. If people did not retire until age 100, and if the increased life span was not based on a series of organ replacements and other super-costly medical procedures, then maybe we might re-examine the 80-year policy.

Q. How is it possible for 25% of the world population in the First World to lift up the standard of living of 75% of the world population in the Third World? Isn't a more likely outcome the living standard of the First World will be dragged down to the level of the Third World?

A. If we do nothing, the standard of the living in the First World will be dragged down in any event. When Uniworld has been attained, which will take 100-200 years, everyone will have a good standard of living. With a 2 billion population, a healthy environment, a world without war, and an efficient, no-frills economy, there will be enough for all.

Q. Where is the incentive for progress?

A. What kind of "progress" do you mean? If you mean bigger houses, bigger cars, 50 pair of shoes, Uniworld does not view this as progress. Uniworld aims for a good standard of living for everyone, but mindless consumerism is not progress. Uniworld substitutes personal development and the satisfying use of leisure time as a more worthwhile goal.

We Can Save The World: *The Uniworld Plan*

Q. The 5-year plans of the former Soviet Union was a colossal failure. Why do you think the proposed Uniworld economy will fare better?
A. The Soviet 5-year plan was a rigidly controlled economy. The Uniworld economy is a free-market profit-driven economy. The role of government in Uniworld is not to control the economy but to keep it functioning smoothly without artificial price control, monopolies, misrepresentation, and avoidable waste and inefficiencies. One difference is that Uniworld will adjust hours of work to avoid both unemployment and labor shortages.

Q. Do you think all the diverse groups throughout the world will willingly erase their ethnic identity?
A. With a world government, arbitrary national boundaries will disappear and people will be able to move about much more freely. When diverse people live together harmoniously they naturally inter-marry. When all groups are treated equally without discrimination, there is less resistance to inter-marriage. Uniworld will not compel inter-marriage but will encourage it by financial and other incentives. The first inter-marriage is the big step; second generation inter-marriages are much easier.

Q. The Uniworld you propose is worse than boring. Everyone will look alike, dress alike, talk alike, live in the same kind of city, in the same kind of house, with the same kind of furniture. What happened to human individuality?
A. This is not entirely true. They may have similar skin color, but some will be young, some old, some short, some tall. People will not dress alike, though clothes will not be discarded simply because of arbitrary change of fashion. But these are all external superficialities. Human individuality is internal: it's personality, achievements, life experiences and character.

Q. How do you expect to get popular support for a program that will take 100-200 years to implement? The people living now make the sacrifice, but the benefit goes to those living 200 years in the future.

A. Not so. Even though it will take 100-200 years to fully implement Uniworld, some of the benefits will start to be apparent in perhaps 20 years. And conversely if we do nothing, deterioration in our standard of living and quality of life will become increasingly apparent starting perhaps 20 years from now. For older people, 70 years and up, it will make little difference. They will be dead and gone before any material change is apparent, but for those less than 50 years of age, what happens in the next 30-60 years will seriously affect them. And the elderly will be concerned about the welfare of grandchildren, even if they themselves are not directly affected.

Q. Isn't the Uniworld Plan a gross infringement of personal freedom, 1984 reborn?

A. Complete freedom is not possible in a civilized society. Even primitive tribes have restrictions and taboos. Civil codes and criminal codes are necessary restrictions on personal behavior. Uniworld will be a democratic society with the right to vote, freedom of speech, freedom of religion, and similar civil liberties as we now enjoy. Uniworld will encourage inter-marriage and ethnic blending by education and incentives, not by force. The Uniworld economy will discourage high cost luxury goods not by prohibition but by tax policy. The only difference is the restriction on having as many children as you choose, and on longevity. In exchange you will have an egalitarian society, with equal treatment for all, a good standard of living for everyone now and in the future, and freedom from fear of war.

How we achieved Uniworld

The year is 2130 and the Uniworld Plan, though not entirely complete, is well on its way. We began Uniworld in 2030, so it's been 100 years. Since 2002 it was apparent to many the world was heading for a serious survival crisis and something along the lines of Uniworld had to be done, but the general public was not yet ready for such a drastic change.

Meanwhile conditions in the Third World were near chaos. With loss of top-soil, salinization, desertification, and depletion of aquifers after three years of record breaking drought, crop yields had declined severely and there was widespread starvation in Africa, India, and elsewhere. Although the major First World countries had so far been able to avoid war, the Third World was in turmoil with food riots, breakdown of civil government, and four wars between neighboring countries competing for dwindling resources.

Desperate Third World countries appealed to the First World for help, but the need was so vast, the First World was unable and unwilling to assist. Their priority was how to secure their borders to block millions of starving people from pouring across. But the starving people were not going to fade away quietly. Their attitude was if you are not going to help us, we'll take you down with us.

Terrorism became widespread everywhere in the First World with small scale bombings and poison gas releases almost daily events. Many were pre-announced and most were hoaxes but the overall effect was devastating to the economies of the First World. But worst was yet to come. It was acknowledged that substantial amounts of weapon grade nuclear material had escaped from Russia by bribery and theft, and was now in the hands of at least a dozen terrorist groups in five or more Third World countries. Although denied officially, most of these terrorist groups were government backed. The terrorists didn't view themselves as international criminals, but rather as patriots fighting for the survival of their families and fellow countrymen.

Up to now, the terrorism had been relatively small scale and intended mostly as a warning, but now they threaten a much higher level of attack. A one-kiloton nuclear bomb can be made with just one pound of plutonium. One pound of plutonium is enough to contaminate the ground water supply of an entire country. In addition to radioactive weapons, they have, or can readily make, chemical weapons such as hydrogen cyanide and sarin, a nerve gas, and biologic weapons such as anthrax. It is impossible to protect thousands of potential targets against a determined attack. The terrorists had these deadly weapons, the means of delivering them, and the will to use them.

This was the state of the world when an emergency session of the United Nations met in Lucerne, Switzerland, in February 2029. The Uniworld Plan was proposed, but soon met an impasse.

A key provision of the Uniworld Plan is a world government and a single worldwide economy. This was unacceptable to the First World countries because the result would be a drastic decline it its standard of living.

After four months of heated debate a solution was found. Instead of starting Uniworld with a worldwide government, we would merge the 185 countries into eight groups, called Uniregions, each an independent sovereign country.

An extensive analysis and study was made to determine the most suitable groupings to make up each regional government. Geographic proximity and similar level of standard of living were important factors and it was also desirable for each Uniregion to have enough agricultural land to be self-sufficient. An effort was made for ethnic and racial diversity in each region since racial and ethnic inter-marriage was one of the goals of Uniworld.

Each Uniregion was to be a sovereign nation, make its own laws, manage its own economy, collect its own taxes, pay for and operate its own social security and health insurance plans, and carry out all the usual functions of an independent nation. Instead of 185 nations, we would now have eight Uniregions. Representatives of each of the eight Uniregions would form the new United Nations and would decide on and administer programs and projects that affected more than one region.

Since the new Uniregions were formed of countries with roughly similar standard of living, the First World countries were in different Uniregions from the Third World countries, and the wide disparity between the First and Third World would continue. If all the countries had been merged into one, with one economy, the standard of living of the First World countries would have drastically declined. The long range plan was to improve the standard of living of the Third World

Uniregions, bring them up to the level of the First World and then merge all the Uniregions into one Uniworld. However it was necessary to start in 2030 with separate Uniregions in order to win the approval of the First World countries.

As might be expected, another major problem was money. The Third World was poor, and it was apparent from the start that they would need substantial financial and technical assistance from the First World but where was the money coming from?

The First World countries did not have surplus funds; most were operating at budget deficits. The most likely source of funds was in the military budget of each country. If all the countries, First World and Third World, disbanded their military forces, this would make substantial funds available. In some of the Third World countries more than 30% of government expenditures is for the military. Russia and China resisted this proposal at first but eventually were persuaded to agree. During the transition period, the United Nations would have a moderate size military force to deal with possible rene-gade countries.

This would be a major commitment extending over at least 50 years. Why would the First World do this? As it is said, charity begins at home, and the First World would certainly have preferred to use the money within its own country, but it had no choice. Population was continuing to mushroom in the Third World, along with destruction of the environment, accompanied by famine and many local wars, and now terrorism in the First World on a huge scale. In return, as a very critical condition to this assistance, the Third World Uniregions agreed to initiate aggressive programs to stop population growth and protect the environment.

And why did the Third World countries agree to the Uniregion/Uniworld Plan? They agreed because the First World would cancel the indebtedness they owe to the First World and would also pro-vide substantial long-term financial and technical assistance to improve their standard of living.

Assistance for the Third World was to focus on providing the basic necessities of living - food, clothing, shelter, medical care, and education. This included clean water, sanitation, sound agricultural practices, good simple housing, small scale industry for making clothing, and other projects to improve standard of living for everyone.

Although the eight Uniregions were separate governments and separate economies, with different standards of living, many of the principles of Uniworld could be initiated at once. Each region was required to limit population and protect the environment. Each would improve its economy by improving efficiency, directing production to basic needs, discouraging luxuries, consumerism, advertising, monopolies, misrepresentation, and marketing gimmicks.

In 2030 we started with eight Uniregions. As the standard of living improved in the poorest, we were able to combine two Uniregions in 2084, another four in 2096, and then finally five years ago in 2125, all the Uniregions were combined into one Uniworld, so now we truly have a world government.

When the Uniworld/Uniregion Plan started in 2030, world population was 9 billion. Despite aggressive efforts to check population growth, it increased to 10 billion because of large numbers of young persons nearing age of parenting. To lower population in some reasonable time span, a one-child policy was needed, but the best we could do the first 20 years was a 1.6 average fertility rate. Since then we have had a fairly effective one-child policy, and population is now, in 2130, 3.5 billion. We still plan to reduce population to 2 billion, but we are now relaxing family size limits to 1.6 fertility rate that will permit many 2-child families.

We have also made strenuous efforts to protect the environment but with only partial success. The pressure from the 10 billion population was overwhelming, but as the population is now declining toward 2 billion we hope to see substantial recovery of environmental health within the next 50 years.

We have a common language, primarily with roots in English but drawing much from other languages. Racial and ethnic blending is 80%

complete; in several more generations differences will not be discernible, so we will no longer need to contend with the troublesome issues of affirmative action, discrimination, unequal opportunity, school busing, and a minority underclass.

After a somewhat rocky start, the no-frills, back-to-basics, free-market economy is now working well. The economy stresses the efficient production of basic goods and services and discourages production of luxuries by a substantial sales tax. Economic waste is reduced by restrictions on advertising, marketing gimmicks, monopolies, proliferation of container sizes, forced obsolescence, and unwarranted litigation.

The cash-less monetary system and the highly sophisticated computer network that records all transactions provides valuable timely information of industry-wide production, sales and inventory and avoids wide swings in the business cycle. Once we reach our 2 billion population, we will have a stable, no-growth economy, requiring little variation from year to year in production volume, making it possible to fine-tune industrial operations.

Equally important to producing an adequate and balanced supply of basic goods and services is assuring adequate purchasing power. We have full employment in Uniworld; if productivity improves, we simply reduce standard working hours per week but with same total pay. The net effect is to increase leisure time. The universal social security system and the universal health care system assures adequate purchasing power for the non-working population: young children, the sick, the disabled, and the retired.

The world government is able to provide liberal social security and health care benefits because the Uniworld Plan provides substantial cost savings. With a world government we save the very high cost of maintaining a military force and repairing the destruction of war. By eliminating government debt we have saved the high annual interest cost.

We have much less crime because the social security safety net has reduced the motivation for crime and the cash-less monetary system makes it easier to trace criminals.

Oil and natural gas have been exhausted many years ago except for a small government holding reserved for restricted special use. The large supply of coal still on hand is not used because of the air pollution it causes, but mostly because it is no longer needed. Our primary energy has been photovoltaic solar ever since research doubled its former efficiency.

We have also made great gains in genetics and have eliminated almost all genetic defects in new-born babies. Now most everyone has a reasonable expectation of good health into the 70's, and that has substantially reduced the cost of the universal health insurance system. We still have a drug problem, but methods of treating and preventing drug addiction are continually improving.

We have accomplished little yet in converting our cities to the standard 100,000 size. We will need 20,000 and so far we have completed less than 2000, because we had been coping with a population of 10 billion. The concept appears sound however and we expect to make substantial headway the next 30 years.

With the increasing leisure time, more and more attention is being given to developing a wide range of programs, physical and intellectual, for recreation, for individual personal development and for those that bring people together in community activities. We also encourage everyone to participate as a volunteer in some worthwhile civic and community service.

Although it has been necessary to make modifications in a few of the provisions of the original Uniworld Plan, so far the Uniworld Plan has been working quite well.

The Choice is Yours

Now let's return to the here and now. We must wake up and acknowledge we have a major problem that we must deal with now. We know the problem and we know, at least in a general way, what we can do about it. Time is of the essence, to quote legalese. The longer we delay taking necessary action, the more severe will be the consequences and the longer it will take to counter it and the greater the needed sacrifice. The solution is the Uniworld Plan, or something very similar, and it will be the same solution whether we start next year or in 50 years. But it will be far more difficult if we start in 50 years than if we start next year. If we start in 1998, we have a population of 6 billion to contend with, but if we wait 50 years, we will have a population of 11 billion.

Paul Ehlich and others sounded the alarm about the population over thirty years ago, when the population was 3.5 billion, but we took no heed. We can't go back thirty years, but we should not delay another 50 years. The additional time makes the task much more difficult.

Let's estimate how long it would take to reduce the population to 2 billion if we start with a population of ll billion. The population is reduced by reducing the average family size below the replacement rate. The China one-child policy is a fertility rate of 1.0. We'll make the estimate using a fertility rate of 1.0 and also using a more realistic rate of 1.6. We will assume an average life span of 80 years and an initial distribution of ages skewed somewhat to the younger ages, which is more realistic than assuming the same 12.5% for all 10-year age brackets:

0-10 years	16.25%
10-20	15.25
20-30	14.25
30-40	13.25
40-50	11.75
50-60	10.75
60-70	9.75
70-up	8.75
total	100.00%

The table below shows the approximate number of years to reduce the population, starting at 11, 10, 8 and 6 billion, and a fertility rate of 1.0 and 1.6:

Years to Reduce Population

billion	fertility 1.0				fertility 1.6			
	11	10	8	6	11	10	8	6
10	38				68			
9	48	40			78	68		
8	54	50			97	82		
7	65	61	42		112	102	72	
6	72	70	56		135	125	95	
5	78	75	67	47	162	150	117	78
4	89	85	75	64	193	180	150	106
3	102	95	87	75	230	217	187	150
2	118	110	105	92	285	270	245	200

According to the above table, starting with a population of 11 billion, and using a fertility rate of 1.0, to reduce the population to 10 billion, will take 38 years. To reduce population to 2 billion will take 118 years. If we use a fertility rate of 1.6, which is more realistic, it will take 285 years to reduce population to 2 billion!

Summarizing, to reduce population to 2 billion:

starting with 11 billion - fertility rate	1.0	118 years
	1.6	285
6 billion - fertility rate	1.0	92
	1.6	200

These are scary numbers - 285 years to reduce population from 11 billion to 2 billion - and this is probably an optimistic estimate. The needed reduction in fertility is almost entirely in Third World countries, many now with fertility rates over 4.0. Here a large family is a matter of pride and a way to provide for old age care. To get voluntary compliance to a 1.6 fertility rate will be virtually impossible.

Worse yet, during this long stretch of time, the environment is deteriorating. We have assumed that a sustainable population level is 2 billion, and anything above that is degrading the environment. So after the

285 years needed to reduce the population, we will need another 285 years to restore the environment. With these kinds of numbers, the outlook is very bleak.

Perhaps we are setting too ambitious a goal. Our objective is 2 billion, but if we bring it down from 11 billion to 6 billion that would be quite an achievement. Maybe we need to set 6 billion as an interim goal, catch our breath at that level, and then gradually in subsequent years bring it down to 2 billion.

Referring again to the table for 1.6 fertility:
from 11 billion to 6 billion - 135 years
8 billion to 6 billion - 95 years
6 billion to 6 billion - 51 years

The 51 years to go from 6 billion to 6 billion needs an explanation. Because the age distribution is skewed toward young people of pre-parenting age, the population will grow to about 6.4 billion the first 30 years, even with full compliance of 1.6 fertility, and then gradually decline back to 6 billion, overall about 51 years. Of course without the 1.6 fertility restriction, the population would be on its way to 11 billion and more.

These are frightening figures. It points out why it is so important to take aggressive action now with a present population of 5.8 billion. If a fire breaks out in your home, the quicker the fire department arrives, the easier the task and the less the damage. Our world is on fire.

These are the choices:
Choice A: There is no problem. This is a big fuss about nothing.
Choice B: There might be a problem later, but it's not very much now. If it becomes a problem, we'll deal with it then.
Choice C: It is just another problem to add to the list. We have many more important things to deal with.
Choice D: Might be a problem later, but I'll be dead and gone by that time.
Choice E: It looks like a serious problem, but not much we can do.

The world will never accept the Uniworld Plan.

Choice F. It looks like a serious problem and we should give it immediate attention. I'm not sure the Uniworld Plan is the answer, but we need to do something.

A principal difference between Man and other animals is that Man has the intelligence to anticipate future events and take appropriate action.

THE CHOICE IS YOURS.

APPENDIX A
BIBLIOGRAPHY

Newspapers and periodicals

Los Angeles Times
Newsweek magazine
Time magazine
Futurist magazine
Technology Review
World Watch

Publications of following organizations

Zero Population Growth
Negative Population Growth
Population Institute
Population Communication International
International Planned Parenthood
Alan Guttmacher Institute
World Federalist Association
United Nations Association
Cousteau Society
Sierra Club
AVSC International
Pathfinder International
Union of Concerned Scientists

Encyclopedias

Encyclopedia Americana
Encyclopedia Britannica
McGraw Hill Encyclopedia of Science and Technology

Books

1. More, Sir Thomas (1516) Utopia.
2. Huxley, Aldous (1932) Brave New World.
3. Bellamy, Edward (1888) Looking Backward.
4. Wells, H.G.(1905) A Modern Utopia.
5. Orwell, George (1949) Nineteen Eighty-Four.
6. Skinner, B.F. (1948) Walden Two.
7. Morris, William (1890) News From Nowhere.
8. Kateb, George (1972) Utopia and Its Enemies.
9. Kumar, Krishan (1991) Utopianism.
10. Kumar, Krishan (1987) Utopia and Anti-Utopia in Modern Times
11. Schumacher, E.F.(1973) Small Is Beautiful.
12. Daly, Herman E.(1991) Steady-State Economics.
13. Holmberg, Johan (Editor)(1992) Making Development Sustainable.
14. Smith, Dennis (1990) Capitalist Democracy on Trial.
15. Boyer, Wm H.(1984) America's Future: Transition to the 21st Century.
16. Lavoie, Don (1985) National Economic Planning: What Is Left?
17. Branch, Melville C.(1990) Planning: Universal Process.
18. Rifkin, Jeremy (1989) Entropy: Into the Greehouse World.
19. Goldin, Augusta (1988) Small Energy Sources.
20. Taylor & Francis (1989) Energy Issues and Options For Developing Countries.
21. Gever, John, et al (1986) Beyond Oil.
22. Ramage, Janet (1983) Energy, A Guidebook.
23. Pilzer, Paul Zane (1990) Unlimited Wealth.
24. Allen, Irving Lewis (editor)(1977) New Towns and the Suburban Dream.
25. Kamarack, Andrew M.(1983) Economics and the Real World.
26. Short, John R.(1989) The Humane City: Cities As If People Matter.
27. Stwertka, Eve and Albert (1989) Genetic Engineering.
28. McCuen, Gary E.(1991) Ending War Against the Earth.

29. Fischer, Claude S.(1984) The Urban Experience.
30. Fowler, Edmund P.(1992) Building Cities That Work.
31. World Book Encyclopedia (1987) The Planet Earth.
32. Gore, Al (1992) Earth in the Balance.
33. Singer, Sam (1985) Human Genetics.
34. Manuel, Rank E.(ed)(1966) Utopias and Utopian Thought.
35. Spann, Edward K.(1989) Brotherly Tomorrows.
36. Long, Robert E.(ed)(1989) Energy and Conservation.
37. U.S.Congress (1991) Energy Technology Choices: Shaping Our Future.
38. Kennedy, Paul (1993) Preparing for the Twenty-First Century.
39. Richter, Peyton (ed)(1975) Utopia/Dystopia.
40. McCord, William (1989) Voyages to Utopia.
41. Brenna, James R.(1985) Patters of Human Heredity.
42. Manuel, Frank and Fritzie (1979) Utopian Thought in the Western World.
43. Time-Life Books (1990) Utopian Visions.
44. Heilbroner, Robert L.(1980) The Wordly Philosophers.
45. Heilbroner, Robert L.(1985) The Making of Economic Society.
46. Bowden, Elbert V.(1974) Economics Through the Looking Glass.
47. Blinder, Alan S.(1987) Hard Heads, Soft Hearts.
48. Drucker, Peter F.(1989) The New Realities.
49. Reich, Robert B.(1992) The Work of Nations.
50. Leone, Bruno (ed)(1986) Capitalism: Opposing Viewpoints.
51. Fusfeld, Daniel R.(1986) Age of the Economist.
52. Wessels, Walter J.(1987) Economics.
53. Stein, Herbert (1992) Illustrated Guide to the American Economy.
54. Sil, Leonard (1986) Economics in Plain English.
55. Carson, Robert B.(1987) Micro-Economic Issues Today.
56. Galbraith, John Kenneth (1987) Economics in Perspective.
57. Harrison, Benet and Bluestone, Harry (1988) The Great U-Turn.
58. McConnell, Campbell R.(1987) Economics (l0th ed).
59. Bender and Leone (ed)(1986) Economics in America, Opposing Viewpoints.
60. Bender and Leone (ed)(1990) Genetic Egineering, Opposing

Viewpoints.

61. Viljoen, Stephan (1974) Economic Systems in World History.
62. Reynolds, Lloyd G.(1982) Macro Economics (4th edition).
63. Miller, Roger LeRoy (1988) Economics Today (6th ed).
64. Bucholz, Todd G.(1989) New Ideas From Dead Economists.
65. McConnell (1980) Ideas of the Great Economists.
66. Pollack, Steve (1993) Ecology.
67. Time-Life Books (1993) Plant Life.
68. Hecht, Jeff (1993) Vanishing Life.
69. Baumol, Wm and Blinder, Alan (1991) Macroeconomics (5th edition).
70. Baumol, Wm and Blinder, Alan (1991) Microeconomics (5th edition).
71. Skousen, Mark (1991) Economics on Trial.
72. Zycher, Benjamin and Lewis, Solmon (ed)(1993) Economic Policy, Financial Markets, and Economic Growth.
73. Goodland, Robert, et al (ed)((1992) Population, Technology, and Life Style.
74. Stead, Edward and Jean (1992) Management For a Small Planet.
75. Burrows, Brian, et al (1991) Into the 21st Century.
76. Cogan, John et al (1994) The Budget Puzzle.
77. Calleo, David P. (1992) The Bankrupting of America.
78. Schell, Jonathan (1982) The Fate of the Earth.
79. Moment, Gairdner B. and Kraushaar, Otto (ed) (1980) Utopias: the American Experience.
80. Kephart, William M.(1987) Extraordinary Groups.
81. Oved, Yaacov (1988) Two Hundred Years of American Communes.
82. Commission on Developing Countries (1992) For Earth's Sake.
83. Kane, Hal (1992) Time For Change.
84. O'Connor, Martin (ed)(1994) Is Capitalism Sustainable?
85. Brown, Lester R.(ed)(1991) World-Watch Reader on Global Environment Issues.
86. Ehrlich, Anne H. and Birks, John W.(ed) (1990) Hidden Dangers.
87. Caplan, Ruth (ed)(1990) Our Earth, Ourselves.
88. Heilbroner, Robert L. and Galbraith, James K.(1987) Understanding Micro-Economics (8th edition).

89. Aaseng, Nathan (1991) Ending World Hunger.
90. James, Peter and Thorpe, Nick (1994) Ancient Inventions.
91. McCrum and Cran and MacNeil (1986) The Story of English.
92. Hailstones, Thomas and Mastrianna, Frank (1988) Basic Economics (8th edition).
93. Ehrlich, Paul R. (1968) The Population Bomb.
94. The Global Tomorrow Coalition - Corson, Walter H.(ed) (1990) The Global Ecology Handbook.
95. Ferencz, Benjamin and Keyes, Ken (1991) Planethood.

APPENDIX B

The following article, "Ehrlich's Fables", written by Paul R Ehrlich and Anne H Ehrlich of Stanford University, first appeared in the January 1997 issue of Technology Review (MIT) and was adapted from their recent book *Betrayal of Science and Reason*. It is reprinted here with the kind permission of the authors.

Both of the authors have written extensively on the subject of the environment and population. Paul R Ehrlich was an early voice calling attention to the danger of a rapidly growing population with his book *The Population Bomb,* published in 1968, about 30 years ago.

Ehrlich's Fables

When polled, 65% of U.S. citizens said they are willing to pay good money for environmental protection, but at the same time most do not believe that environmental deterioration is a crucial issue in their own lives. This seeming contradiction may stem from the fact that it is difficult to recognize subtle and gradual environmental change. But it may also stem from another fact: that various sources, including conservative think tanks such as the Cato Institute and the Heritage Foundation, have been disseminating erroneous information regarding the true state of the environment. Adam Myerson, editor of the Heritage Foundation's Policy Review, pretty much summed up this viewpoint in the journal when he maintained that "leading scientists have done major work disputing the current henny-pennyism about global warming, acid rain, and other purported environmental catastrophes."

A flood of recent books and articles have also advanced the notion that all is well with the environment after giving undue prominence to the opinions of one or a handful of contrarian scientists in the name of "sound science" and "balance". With strong and appealing messages, these authors have successfully sowed the seeds of doubt among policymakers and the public about the reality and importance of phenomena such as overpopulation, global climate change, ozone depletion, and loss of biodiversity.

If U.S. citizens were convinced that some changes could enhance their quality of life and that of their children, most would gladly oblige. But when the necessity of such changes is questioned, especially in the name of science and reason, it's not surprising that most people are hesitant to embark on the necessary course to tackle environmental problems.

What follows is a sampling of the myths, or fables, that the promoters of "sound science" and "balance" are promulgating about issues relating to population and food, the atmosphere and climate, toxic substances, and economics and the environment. By looking at them through the lens of the present scientific consensus, we aim to reveal the gross errors on which they are founded. Thus we may return to higher ground and engage in a crucial dialogue about how to sustain the environment.

Fables and Population and Food

Myth: There is no overpopulation today because the Earth has plenty of room for more people.

In fact, humanity has already overshot Earth's carrying capacity by a simple measure: no nation is supporting its present population on a steady flow of renewable resources. Rich agricultural soils are being eroded in many areas at rates of inches per decade, though such soils are normally formed at rates of inches per millennium. Accumulations of "fossil" fresh water, stored underground over thousands of years during glacial periods, are being mined as if they were metals - and often for low-value uses such as irrigating forage crops like alfalfa, for grazing animals. Water from these aquifers, which are recharged at rates measured in inches per year, is being pumped out in feets per year. And species and populations of organisms, plants, and other animals are being exterminated at a rate unprecedented in 65 million years - on the order of 10,000 times faster than they can be replaced by the evolution of new genes.

Myth: We needn't worry about population growth in the United States because it's not nearly as densely populated as other countries.

The idea that the number of people per square mile is a key determinant of population pressure is as widespread and persistent as it is wrong. In Apocalypse Not, published by the Cato Institute, economist Ben Bolch and chemist Harold Lyons point out that if the 1990 world population were placed in Texas, less than half of 1 percent of the Earth's land surface, "each person would have an area equal to the floor space of the typical U.S. home". They also say: "Anyone who has looked out an airplane window while traveling across the country knows how empty the United States really is."

But the key issue in judging overpopulation is not how people can fit into any given space but whether the Earth can supply the population's long-term requirements for food, water, and other resources. Most of the "empty" land in the United States either grows the food essential to the well-being of the world (as in Iowa), supplies us with forestry products (as in northern Maine), or, lacking water, good soil, and a suitable climate, cannot contribute directly to the support of civilization (as in much of Nevada). The point is that densely populated countries such as the Netherlands, Bermuda, and Monaco and cities such as Singapore, Sao Paulo, Mexico City, Tokyo, and New York can be crowded with people only because the rest of the world is not.

Myth: We should have a bigger population for no other reason than that "people like to be alive."

One can respond to such statements by asking, "Would people like to be alive if they had live like chickens in a factory farm? But such retorts are unnecessary. The best way to maximize the number of Americans (or Chinese or Nigerians) who live wouldn't be to cram as many of them as possible into these countries in the next few decades until they self-destruct. Rather, it is to have permanently sustainable populations in those nations for tens of thousands, perhaps millions, of years.

Myth: We need a larger population so we will have more geniuses to solve our environmental problems.

Having additional people to work on problems does not necessarily lead to solutions. Consider what happened to the people of Easter Island after this lush, 64-square-mile subtropical Pacific island, some 2,000 miles west of Chile, was colonized by Polynesians some 1,500 years ago. Even as the population soared to around 20,000, all those minds couldn't solve the tiny island's resource problems. The large forest of towering palm trees that graced the land was harvested more rapidly than it regenerated. Once they were gone, there was no way to build canoes for porpoise hunting, and without the forest to absorb and meter out rainfall, streams and springs dried up, unprotected soil eroded away, crop yields dropped, and famine struck the once-rich island. Unlike most premodern peoples, the islanders apparently didn't limit their fertility. Instead, as food supplies became short, they switched to cannibalism, which turned out to be an effective - if not very attractive - method of population control. A common curse became, "The flesh of your mother sticks between my teeth."

Can't today's population, with its knowledge of the history of past civilizations and billions of working minds, help us avoid the fate of the Easter Islanders, and the Henderson Islanders (who completely died out on one of the Pitcairn islands in the South Pacific), the classic Mayans, the Anasazi (native Americans who built the vast pueblos of Chacon County), and others who destroyed the environmental supports of their societies? We wish the answer were yes. Yet the billions of minds we have today are not stopping society from destroying its resources even faster than earlier civilizations destroyed theirs.

But that aside, perhaps the larger point is that environmental rather than genetic differences determine what proportion of a population will display genius. It's very hard to become the next Mozart if one is starving to death on the outskirts of Port-au-Prince. Having more people today is not the solution for generating more geniuses. Creating environment in which the inherent talents of people now disadvantaged - by race or gender discrimination, poverty, or malnutrition - can be fully expressed, is.

Myth: Feeding the world's population is a problem of distribution, not supply.

Of course, if everyone shared food resources equally, and no grain were fed to animals, all of humanity could be adequately nourished today. Unfortunately, such scenarios are irrelevant. Although people in the developed countries could eat lower on the food chain - that is by consuming less meat and more grain - and might be willing to make such sacrifices to improve the environment, it is unrealistic to think we will all suddenly become vegetarian saints as is to think we will suddenly trade in our cars for bicycles, or go to bed at sunset to save energy.

But even if everyone were willing to eat a largely vegetarian diet today, with only a small supplement from fish and range-fed animals, and food were equitably distributed to everyone, today's harvest could feed about 7 billion of such altruistic vegetarians, according to calculations by the Alan Shawn Feinstein World Hunger Program at Brown University and our group, the Center for Conservation Biology, at Stanford. Since the world's population is nearly 6 billion already. this is hardly a comforting number.

Myth: We needn't worry about future food supplies because scientific break-throughs (as yet unimagined) will boost grain yields around the world.

Analyses of food-production trends over the past few decades suggest that there certainly is cause to worry about maintaining food supplies. While it is true that the most important indicator of human nutrition, world grain production, has roughly tripled since 1950, what food optimists overlook is that the Green Revolution has already been put in place in most suitable areas, and most of the expected yield gains have been achieved. Consequently, grain production increases have failed to keep up with population growth since 1985, and we've seen no productivity gains in absolute terms since 1990. Meanwhile, grain reserves have shrunk severely. A new kit of tools to expand food production is required to carry us into the future, yet no such kit appears to be on the horizon. And even if some unanticipated breakthrough were to be made, it would take years if not decades to develop and deploy new crop varieties - years during which demand would continue rising as the population expanded.

Fables About the Atmosphere and Climate
Myth: There is no evidence that global warming is real.

The climatic system is exceedingly complex and entirely understood, but some facts are indisputable. First, scientists have known for more than a century that releasing carbon dioxide could add to the greenhouse effect caused by the gaseous composition of Earth's atmosphere. The atmosphere contains an array of natural greenhouse gases - including water vapor, carbon dioxide, and methane - that are relatively transparent to the incoming short-wavelength energy of sunlight but relatively opaque to the long-wavelength infrared energy radiated upward by the sunlight-warmed earth. The greenhouse gas and clouds together absorb most of this outgoing infrared energy and reradiate some of it back towards the Earth, thus functioning as a heat-trapping blanket over the planet. The naturally occurring concentrations of these gases are enough to raise the Earth's average surface temperature to about 59 degrees F. Without greenhouse gases, it would be about zero degrees, the oceans would be frozen to the bottom. and life as we know it would be impossible

Second, scientists also know that humanity is adding to the greenhouse effect - that the atmospheric concentration of carbon dioxide in 1992 was some 30 percent above preindustrial levels, and the concentration of methane has increased by 145 percent. Both gases are natural atmospheric constituents whose concentrations have fluctuated substantially in geologic history. But analyses of air trapped in ice cores from the Antarctic and Greenland ice caps show that today's levels are by far the highest concentrations of these greenhouse gases in at least the last 160,000 years. Moreover, nitrous oxide, another greenhouse gas, has increased about 15 percent over its preindustrial level. And chlorofluorocarbons (CFCs) - the ozone-destroying chemicals - also contribute to the greenhouse effect.

Thermometers worldwide have documented nearly a full 1-degree rise since the nineteenth century. Furthermore, a consensus has formed in the climatological community that a "discernible signal" of anthropogenic warming is beginning to emerge from the "noise" of natural climatic variation. In fact, the 1995 report of the scientific committee of the Intergovernmental Panel on Climate Change (IPCC) stated based on the warming record over the past century, and especially in recent decades, "the balance of evidence suggests that there is a discernible human influence on global climate."

Myth: Global warming exists only in computer simulations.

The IPCC's conclusion was, indeed, based primarily on a new generation of computer simulations. But the results were also based on detailed comparisons with actual temperature records. Moreover, the total body of evidence that the planet is warming is now overwhelming. For example, surface-temperature records, even when corrected for the effect of urban "heat islands" (areas artificially heated by structures such as buildings and parking lots), show that the ten warmest years in the past 140 years have all occurred since 1980. And the most recent satellite measurements show that shrinkage in Arctic sea ice, another expected result of global warming, accelerated significantly between 1987 and 1994.

Myth: Even if the concentration of carbon dioxide doubled, since it is responsible for only 1 percent of the greenhouse effect it wouldn't contribute to global warming.

By itself, a doubling of CO_2 (which, incidentally, accounts for some 10 to 25 percent of the natural greenhouse effect, not 1 percent) would warm Earth by less than 2 degrees. But therein lies the power of positive feedback. A 2-degree rise in temperature would cause more water to evaporate from the oceans and thus contribute additional water vapor to the greenhouse effect, resulting in a final warming that most climatologists project to be a little less than 4 degrees. But if the complicating ice and cloud feedbacks are added in, models suggest that anywhere from 3 to 9 degrees of warming would result from a doubling in CO_2 levels. Scientists cannot make more accurate predictions at the moment because of uncertainties surrounding the feedback processes, yet most think the upper limit represents ecological disaster. For example, 9 degrees is about the difference in global average temperature that separates today's climate from that of the last ice age, when the present site of New York City was visited by a mile-thick glacier.

Myth: If the average mean temperature of the world were to rise a few degrees in the next century, we could simply wear lighter clothes and use more air-conditioning.

The idea that the primary reason to be concerned about global warming is that our backyards would be a little hotter during the summer barbecue season is as pervasive as it is wrong. The larger problem is that the climate change could seriously disrupt a food-production system that already is showing signs of stress. Other potential problems include sea level rise, which would cause coastal flooding and salinization of groundwater, as well as more intense storms. Finally, natural ecosystems - our life-support systems - will have great difficulty in adjusting to rapid climate change. The trees in southern forests can't just fly up to New England or put on a lighter shirt when the heat becomes too much for them.

Myth: CFCs can't rise 18 miles into the atmosphere to deplete the ozone layer because they are made from molecules that are 4 to 8 times heavier than air.

This statement reveals an outrageous misconception about the dynamics of the atmosphere. Gases of the atmosphere are not layered like a lasagna. If they were, the lowest few feet of atmosphere would consist of krypton, ozone, nitrous oxide, carbon dioxide, and argon. Above that would be a thick layer of pure oxygen, and above that even a thicker layer of pure nitrogen followed by water vapor, methane, neon, helium, and hydrogen. In fact, the atmosphere undergoes dynamic mixing, dominated by motions of large air masses, which thoroughly mixes light and heavy gas molecules. Because of this mixing, CFCs have been detected in literally thousands of stratospheric air samples by dozens of research groups all over the world.

Myth: The chlorine in CFCs is not likely to deplete the ozone layer because volcanoes pump out 50 times more chlorine annually than an entire year's production of CFCs.

Mount Erebus does pump out 50 times more chlorine per year in the form of hydrogen chloride (HCl) than humanity adds in CFCs. But the statement is irrelevant to depletion of the ozone layer because much of the HCl released by volcanoes is dissolved in the abundant steam that is also emitted and is thus quickly rained out. Unfortunately, unlike HCl, CFCs are not water soluble and thus cannot be washed out of the atmosphere until they have been broken down. And by then, they will have already done their damage to the ozone layer.

Myth: If there were, in fact, some reduction in the ozone layer, we could simply wear more hats and sunscreen to avoid skin cancer.

The direct effects of the thinning of the ozone layer - which include not only increased rates of skin cancer (including lethal melanomas) but also disruption of the immune system - could, of course, be partially avoided by increased use of hats and sunscreens. But rubbing lotions on Earth's plants and animals would be required as well, since the most important threat from ozone depletion is to natural and agricultural ecosystems. Increases of ultraviolet-B radiation could significantly reduce yields of major crops and has been shown to have other significant adverse effects - such as mutation and immune-system impairment - in a wide variety of plants, animals, and microorganisms.

Fables About Toxic Substances
Myth: Without the use of massive quantities of pesticides, starvation would stalk the planet.

The truth is that we are already using far too great a tonnage of pesticides for the results achieved. Humanity now applies about 2.5 million tons of synthetic pesticides worldwide each year, and pesticide production is a multibillion dollar industry. Yet pests and spoilage still destroy 25 to 50 percent of crops before and after harvest. That proportion, if anything, is higher than the average crop losses before synthetic pesticides were widely introduced after World War II.

The strategy of large scale broadcast spraying of pesticides has proven a poor one - except from the standpoint of petrochemical-company profits. An important reason for this lack of success is the rapidity with which pest populations evolve resistance: aided by short generation times and large populations, more than 500 species of insects and mites no longer respond to pesticides, and resistance to herbicides has been noted in more than 100 species of weeds and 150 species of plant pathogens.

Moreover, only a small proportion of the pesticides applied to fields ever actually reaches the target pest. For instance, of those delivered by aerial crop dusters, some 50 to 75 percent miss the target area and less than 0.1 percent may actually reach the pest. The remainder by definition is an environmental contaminant that can injure people and non-target species and in some cases migrate to the far reaches of the globe.

Yet in most cases pests can be effectively controlled without heavy applications of pesticides by using more biologically based methods. Known as integrated pest management (IPM), this approach involves various strategies such as encouraging natural enemies of pests, developing and planting pest-resistant strains of crops, fallowing, mixed cropping, destroying crop wastes where pests shelter, as well as some limited use of pesticides. IPM is generally vastly superior to chemical-based pest control methods from both economic and environmental perspectives.

Indonesia, for example, has had remarkable success with IPM. In 1986, responding to the failure to chemically control the brown planthopper, a presidential decree banned 57 of 66 pesticides used on rice. Pesticide subsidies, which were as high as 80% percent, were phased out over two years, and some of the resources saved were diverted into IPM. Since then, more than 250,000 farmers have been trained in IPM techniques, insecticide use has plunged by 60 percent, the rice harvest has risen more than 15 percent, and farmers and the Indonesian treasury have save more than $1 billion.

Pesticide use no doubt could be greatly reduced everywhere by wider adoption of IPM, which relies on synthetic pesticides as a scalpel only when needed rather than as a bludgeon. Relaxing cosmetic standards on foods (such as allowing signs of minor insect damage) might also lead to reductions in pesticide use, as could the recent shift in public preferences toward "organically grown" foods. In fact, Americans increasingly distrust toxic chemicals, as is indicated by soaring sales of organically grown fruits and vegetables, which doubled to $7.6 billion from 1989 to 1994.

Overall, pesticide use in the United States could be reduced by 50 percent for a negligible increase (less than 1 percent) in food prices, according to calculations made in 1991 by the authors of the Handbook of Pest Management in Agriculture. Such a reduction could prove to be a great bargain if, as some scientists think, exposure to pesticide residue can impair the human immune system. And in view of today's deteriorating epidemiological environment, in which new diseases are emerging and drug-resistant strains of bacteria are causing resurgence of diseases once believed conquered, any loss of immune function should be taken seriously.

Myth: Exposure to dioxin is considered by some experts to be no more risky than spending a week sunbathing.

Of course, with the increase in ultraviolet radiation reaching the Earth's surface because of depletion of the ozone shield, a week of sunbathing is hardly a risk-free activity. But, more seriously, despite a recent barrage of misinformation - plenty of evidence shows that dioxin is a very dangerous chemical, especially in one of its more common forms, known by its chemical shorthand as TCDD.

Dioxin is a byproduct of the combustion of chlorine-containing substances - which are commonly formed when plastics are burned in incinerators and during the manufacture of the herbicide 2,4,5-T - and used in some industrial processes such as bleaching paper. People can absorb tiny amount of dioxin by eating food contaminated by paper containers, by breathing air polluted with emissions from waste incinerators, or handling some herbicides of bleached paper products.

Dioxin is not only easily absorbed and persistent in the body, it is also an extremely potent toxin. As little as one billionth of an ounce can cause chloracne (a severe form of acne) and various generalized complaints such as headaches, dizziness, digestive upsets, and pain. Animal studies and epidemiological investigations indicate that larger doses of dioxin can cause some kinds of cancer. Other effects that have been found include liver and kidney problems, stillbirths, birth defects, and immune suppression. And prenatal exposure to dioxin appears to have a variety of effects on hormone expression - as observed in laboratory animals and wildlife exposed to TCDD - that are sometimes feminizing and sometimes masculinizing.

Fables About Economics and the Environment

Myth: The United States can't afford stronger environmental protection; it would interfere with growth of the gross national product.

In 1990, William K. Reilly, then head of the U.S. Environmental Protection Agency, reported that the direct cost of compliance with federal environmental regulations was more than $90 billion per year - about 1.7 percent of the nation's GNP. But Reilly also pointed out that, during the two decades when the United States made substantial environmental progress, "the GNP increased by more than 70 percent." This, at worst, it seems that environmental regulation may slightly slow growth in the most commonly used measure of economic progress.

But that said, it should be noted there is a growing mistrust of the ability of the GNP to mirror such progress, or more specifically, the enhancement of social well-being assumed to go along with it. In fact, between 1957 and 1992, although US per-capita income doubled, the percentage of people considering themselves "very happy" declined from 35 to 32 percent.

One of the most prominent critics of the GNP as an indicator of well-being has been economist Herman E. Daly of the University of Maryland, formerly with the World Bank. Daly has suggested a new measure of economic well-being, the index of sustainable economic welfare (ISEW), which attempts to incorporate economic factors including depreciation of "natural capital", such as soil lost to erosion, in its calculation. Between 1951 and 1990, the U.S. per-capita GNP in inflation adjusted dollars more than doubled, while the ISEW grew considerably less than 20 percent and actually declined slightly between 1980 and 1990. "Economic welfare has been deteriorating," Daly says, largely because of "the exhaustion of resources and unsustainable reliance on capital from overseas to pay for domestic consumption and investment."

Other nations are also actively seeking better indicators of human satisfaction, especially those that include the critical factor of the depreciation of natural capital, from the microbes that maintain soil fertility to fresh water stored in aquifers. Norway has started accounting for its remaining balances of mineral and living resources. France now has "natural patrimony accounts" that track the status of all resources influenced by human activity. And the Dutch government has instituted an accounting system that includes environmental damage and the cost of repairing it. Sweden, Germany, and the United States are all moving in the same direction, with the U.S. Department of Commerce developing a "green gross domestic product." In short, recognition is growing that once a nation has attained a certain level of individual material comfort, boosting the GNP is no longer a sufficient aim.

Myth: Stricter environmental regulations will cost American jobs by forcing industries to relocate in nations with weaker standards.

Certainly environmental regulations can cost some jobs, especially in extractive industries or when outdated factories are forced to close because the costs of installing emission controls exceeds the value of the plants. It should be noted, though. that some of the industries (such as mining and logging) that complain the loudest about jobs lost to environmental regulations are of the boom-and-bust variety - set to move on anyway when local resources are depleted.

Other companies pressed by regulations may indeed choose to relocate to nations with weaker environmental laws (and cheaper labor). But as they do, other new jobs are often created, such as in high tech businesses that favor areas where environmental quality is high, both because clean air and water are essential for their operations and because a healthy local environment helps them attract skilled labor. Moreover, even if factories required to install pollution-control equipment close down and throw their employees out of work, others will purchase smokestack scrubbers, thus creating jobs in firms that make such equipment. Overall, environmental protection is not a major cause of job losses and can be a significant source of new jobs.

Myth: Economics, not ecology, should guide policy decisions.

A politician who says something like, "The time has come to put the economy ahead of the environment," clearly doesn't understand that the economy is a wholly-owned subsidiary of natural ecosystems, and that the natural environment supplies humanity with an indispensable array of goods and services. In fact, expressed in economic terms, the value of ecosystem services is enormous. For example, the ability of the ecosystem to control pests could be worth $1.4 trillion annually, since without natural pest control there could be no production of agricultural crops. Ecosystem services might be valued at a total of about $20 trillion per year - almost equal to the gross global product. But these valuations only hint at the actual value of the services, for without them there would be no human society to enjoy their unsung benefits.

All economists understand that economics is supposed to seek wise ways to allocate resources to meet human needs. As traditionally practiced, however, economics has often considered only the delivery of conventional goods and services while ignoring environmental goods and services. That economics is not a wise guide for environmental policy decisions is underlined by economists themselves, who say they detect few "signals" indicating serious environmental problems. They are, of course, waiting for price signals reflecting shortages of resources while remaining ignorant of the depletion of many of the most critical resources such as biodiversity, water quality, and the atmosphere's capacity to absorb greenhouse gases without catastrophic consequences, which are not priced by markets.

One Planet, One Experiment

A quick review of some compelling statistics reveals how wrong- and indeed how threatening to humanity's future - proponents of the notion that we have nothing to worry about can be. The roughly 5-fold increase in the number of human beings over the past century and a half is the most dramatic terrestrial event since the retreat of ice-age glaciers thousands of years ago. That explosion in human numbers has been combined with a 4-fold increase in consumption per person and the adoption of a wide array of technologies that needlessly damage the environment. The result is a 20-fold escalation since 1850 of the pressure humanity places on its environment, as indexed by energy use, the best single indicator of society's environmental impact. Despite such ominous trends, the anti-environmental proponents continue to hammer away in print and over the airways, sowing confusion and doubt in the mind of many citizens about the seriousness - if not the very existence - of environmental deterioration. Thus efforts on behalf of the environment have been limited mainly to grassroots initiatives such as curbside recycling, ecotourism, and enthusiasm for anything "organic". While we applaud such endeavors, they are utterly insufficient steps that may divert attention from much more basic issues. Instead, society needs to take a longer view and recognize that to be sustainable, the economy must operate in harmony with Earth's ecosystems.

Civilization's highest priority must be lowering the pressure on those vital ecosystems, seeking a sustainable food-population balance, and safeguarding human health against global toxification and emerging pathogens alike. Achieving this will require humanely reducing the size of populations worldwide by lowering birthrates to below death rates, reducing per capita consumption among the rich to make room for needed growth in consumption among the poor, and adopting more benign technologies.

Global society is running a vast and dangerous experiment. If the experiment goes wrong, there will be no way to rerun it. In the end, we can only hope that science and reason will prevail and that the public and political leaders will heed its warnings.